BISCUIT JOINER
BASICS

Hugh Foster

Sterling Publishing Co., Inc. New York

Dedication

For Dalton Jaeger: After a quarter century as a teacher, one thing I'm certain of is that the best teacher simply lights a fire; thanks to you, I'm burnin'.

Some of the projects which appear in this book have been published in a different form in *Craftsman at Home* and *Popular Woodworking* magazines.

Library of Congress Cataloging-in-Publication Data

Foster, Hugh.
    Biscuit joiner basics / Hugh Foster.
        p.   cm.
    Includes index.
    ISBN 0-8069-0860-2
    1. Wood-cutting tools.   2. Joinery.   I. Title
  TT186.F65   1996
  684′.083—dc20   95-48399
                                                  CIP

1 3 5 7 9 10 8 6 4 2

Published by Sterling Publishing Company, Inc.
387 Park Avenue South, New York, N.Y. 10016
© 1996 by Hugh Foster
Distributed in Canada by Sterling Publishing
⅌ Canadian Manda Group, One Atlantic Avenue, Suite 105
Toronto, Ontario, Canada M6K 3E7
Distributed in Great Britain and Europe by Cassell PLC
Wellington House, 125 Strand, London WC2R 0BB, England
Distributed in Australia by Capricorn Link (Australia) Pty Ltd.
P.O. Box 6651, Baulkham Hills, Business Centre, NSW 2153, Australia
Printed and bound in Hong Kong
All rights reserved

Sterling ISBN 0-8069-0860-2

Contents

Acknowledgments

The following manufacturers and manufacturer representatives lent me tools and provided advice and photos which helped to improve this book:
Bill Austin and Roy Thompson of Makita U.S.A.
Jim Brewer of Freud
Chris Carlson and Sil Argentin of S-B Power Tools
Frank Coots and Nancy Bronson of Ryobi
Larry Greenwood of Hafele
Bob Jardinico of Colonial Saw
John Liu of Börg
Mike Mangan of Sears
Rick Schmitt of Porter-Cable
and Black & Decker/DeWalt/Elu

Mike Cea at Sterling did his usual excellent job of transforming my collection of text, notes, and photos into the book.

Without the help of all these people, this book would not exist. Of course, responsibility for errors and omissions remains my own.

INTRODUCTION

Biscuit joiners are machines used to cut slots in wood in which wooden wafers are inserted. When they were first introduced to the United States market in the 1970s, they were regarded as just another expensive and extravagant gadget. Since then, their price, especially relative to the cost of labor, has become much more reasonable. Today, the biscuit joiner (also frequently referred to as a plate joiner), which can be afforded by the home craftsman and has proven to be very useful, has become as essential to the serious woodworker as the cordless electric drill (Illus. I-1).

The biscuit joiner has not become so popular simply because of its cost. It has several advantages in the workshop. It provides for the accurate alignment of strong joints, and will help make any woodworker more productive.

Although biscuits—the wooden wafers used to join the slots cut by the biscuit joiner—are more expensive than commercial dowels and much

Illus. I-1. *The biscuit joiner has proven to be a very valuable addition to the workshop.*

more expensive than shop-made ones, in today's shop labor costs far exceed material costs when the total cost of the project is determined. Thus, woodworkers have to work quickly, neatly, and efficiently. The joiner will help you considerably in meeting these goals.

Another advantage of the biscuit joiner is that woodworkers can use it to make some kinds of joints they otherwise might have avoided making. For example, I seldom used mitre joints (joints made by assembling boards with ends cut at an angle) in a piece of furniture because they were hard to hold together. Compound mitres were even harder to join, no matter how attractive they might have been. They both can be made very easily and accurately with biscuit joints.

Nearly all assemblies go together more easily when fastened with the joiner rather than by the more conventional methods. It will probably also make the project more affordable for your customers. Illus. I-2 shows a desk organizer that was assembled with no fasteners other than joining biscuits. (See Chapter 11 for complete design and building instructions for this project.) Just a few years ago, this project would have been more difficult to make, much less produce in quantity.

As important as speed and productivity is the issue of safety. After hundreds of hours experimenting with biscuit joiners, I am convinced that they are among the safest of tools, safer than any of the other portable tools with the possible exception of the pad sander. However, like routers, belt sanders, and most other electrically powered tools, biscuit joiners are loud (most of them run just under 95 decibels), so wear hearing protection whenever you use your biscuit joiner. Also, they generate a lot of dust, so use a dust-collection system. (See the safety instructions in Chapter 4.)

In the following pages, you will learn everything needed to operate a biscuit joiner. This includes a look at its different parts, how to select one that best meets your needs, safety and maintenance techniques, and cutting techniques—which include information on laying out your work and ways to make a variety of joints. The last chapter shows you how to use this information to build an array of interesting projects. A glossary is also included which will clarify woodworking terms you may be unfamiliar with. As you will soon learn, the biscuit joiner is a tool you'll use more and more frequently in your workshop.

Hugh Foster

Illus. I-2. *Projects like this handsome desk organizer can be built quickly, thanks to the use of biscuit joinery. This project is described in Chapter 11.*

Chapter I

HOW THE BISCUIT JOINER WORKS

A joiner is a grinder-like device with a spring-loaded faceplate that sets the depth for plunge cuts (Illus. 1-1). Short spurs or rubber face pieces grab the workpiece while the rotating carbide blade plunges through the faceplate to make the right cut for a biscuit. The biscuits work like dowels and splines to help align adjoining surfaces so they are flush with each other. (See the next chapter.)

There are basically two kinds of joiners. The most commonly available one *plunges* straight into its slotting cut (Illus. 1-2). Another kind, of which very few are available, *pivots* into its biscuit-cutting slot (Illus. 1-3). This is basically a disadvantage because the joint layout for this type of joiner isn't as simple or precise as the layout for a plunging joiner, although this kind of joiner is able to make grooving cuts and certain kinds of cutoffs more easily than the plunging joiner. The biscuit joiner has two basic adjustments: one for the depth of the cut, and the other for the location of the cut. These adjustments and other parts of the joiner are discussed below.

Biscuit Joiner Parts

Although the biscuit joiner has fewer parts and is much simpler to operate than most other power tools, an overview of its different components will prove helpful. The *faceplate* is the plate on the front of the joiner. The blade plunges through the faceplate to make the cut for the slot. The *fence* is an attachment at a 90- or 45-degree angle to the joiner's faceplate which helps determine the position of the joiner's slotting cuts.

The *depth-of-cut scale* indicates how deeply the blade will cut. The depth-of-cut scale is marked for numbers 0, 10, and 20 biscuits, and you can quickly adjust it by simply pulling the depth-gauge plunger towards the front of the machine and twisting it to whichever position you desire before returning it to its working position.

The depth-of-cut scale on joiners that plunge straight into the cut can be adjusted with a pair of knurled jamb nuts (Illus. 1-4). Make this fine adjustment every time after you remove the blade cover, and check it periodically. Adjust the depth-of-cut on pivot-cutting joiners by tightening or loosening the depth-of-cut screw to specific places on a scale (Illus. 1-5). A clockwise adjustment makes the depth-of-cut shallower. A counterclockwise rotation makes the cut deeper.

Some biscuit joiners have a more accurate rack-and-pinion adjustment (Illus. 1-6). The *square guides* on the biscuit joiner help to ensure that square joints go together square. The *flap fence* helps to cut accurately positioned slots in angled work. The *spindle lock* permits blade changing with a single wrench. *The spring-loaded centering pins* on plunge joiners help to keep the joiners from moving when you make the plunge cuts. Most biscuit joiners come with a *D-shaped handle*. Woodworkers operate the biscuit joiner by gripping this handle.

Product Data—Plate Joiners

Model number   B1650
Identification number   0 603 228 1 . .
Voltage rating AC•   12V / 50-60Hz
Amperage rating   5.8A
Watts—in   700W
No load RPM (revolutions per minute)   11,000 RPM
Weight   10.0 lbs.

(• = This tool is designed for use with Alternating Current (AC) only.)

Accessory Listing

Chip bag assembly*
Blade*
Case*
Glue bottle*
Vacuum hose
Hose/vacuum adapter

(* = standard equipment)

Plate Joiner Components

1. Slide ON-OFF switch
2. Top handle
3. 3 position depth stop wheel
4. Depth adjustment knob
5. Adjustable front fence
6. Front fence angle lock knobs
7. Front fence angle scale
8. Front fence height lock knobs
9. Ventilation slots
10. Chip bag
11. Chip bag clip
12. Cord
13. Motor housing

14. Anti-slip inserts
15. Screws
16. Blade
17. Blade screw
18. Allen wrench
19. Spindle wrench
20. Base assembly
21. Line of cut indicator
22. Front fence height scale
23. Highlighted centerline
24. Cutting depth scale
25. Depth stop wheel tabs
26. Bag connector
27. Porthole

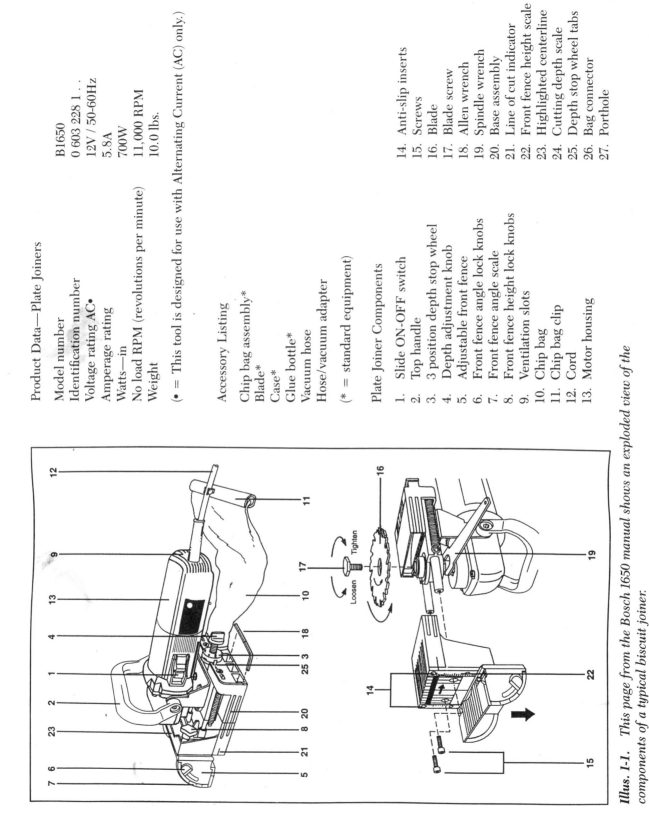

Illus. 1-1. *This page from the Bosch 1650 manual shows an exploded view of the components of a typical biscuit joiner.*

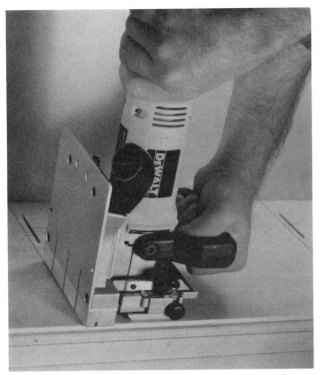

Illus. 1-2. Plunge-cutting joiners plunge straight into their cuts. They are the most commonly available kind of joiner.

Illus. 1-3. Pivot-cutting joiners cut at an angle. This is a disadvantage, although pivot-cutting joiners are able to make certain kinds of cuts more easily than plunging joiners. There are very few pivot-cutting joiners sold on the market today.

Illus. 1-4. The depth-of-cut scale on a plunge-cutting joiner such as this one can be adjusted with a pair of knurled jamb nuts.

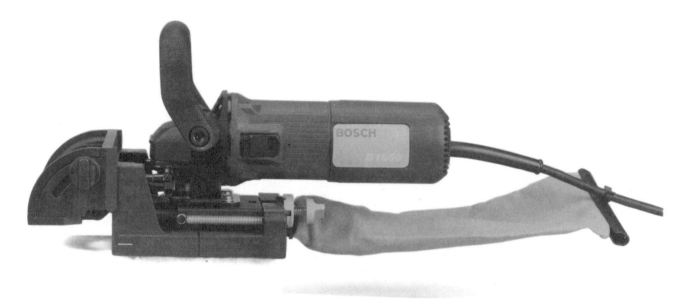

Illus. 1-5.   *The depth-of-cut scale on plunge-cutting joiners can be adjusted by tightening or loosening the depth-of-cut screw at specific places on a scale.*

Rack-and-Pinion Adjustment

Illus. 1-6.   *Some biscuit joiners have a more accurate rack-and-pinion adjustment than others.*

Chapter 2

BISCUITS

After the slots have been cut in two pieces, biscuits (also called plates) are inserted into the pieces and the biscuit joint is assembled. Biscuits are thin, football-shaped wafers. Wooden biscuits are most widely used, although plastic ones are available. (See pages 15–23.) General woodworking biscuits come in three basic sizes (Illus. 2-1), although other sizes are available. A number 0 biscuit is ⅝ inch wide × 1¾ inches long. A number 10 biscuit is ¾ inch wide × 2⅛ inches long. A number 20 biscuit is ¹⁵⁄₁₆ inch wide by 2⅜ inches long. The other sizes, much less commonly available, are discussed on pages 17–19.

Each biscuit is .148 inch thick, and though thinner than the ⁵⁄₃₂-inch blade that cuts the slots, it swells rapidly in contact with moisture to .164 inch, enough to grip the slots tenaciously. When the biscuit is inside the slot, the result is a joint that is very sound mechanically, which is essential. In fact, a biscuit joint after just 20 minutes of clamping is stronger than a dowel or spline joint and as strong as standard mortise-and-tenon joints, which are more difficult to make.

Though some companies insist that their brands of biscuits be used with their joiners, any brand of biscuit will work with any joiner. Illus. 2-2 compares generic, Porter-Cable, and Lamello biscuits, and a Lamello clamping biscuit, which is shown for size comparison.

When first starting out, most woodworkers should buy a package of mixed biscuits, which generally includes 250 each of numbers 0 and 10 biscuits and 500 of number-20 biscuits. Most of us will use all the number-20 biscuits long before using the smaller sizes, and then purchase a box of 1,000 number-20 biscuits. It's a good idea to keep a spare package of the least-expensive brand of number 20-biscuits on hand. You will find yourself using many biscuits, and, if you do not live in the city, you will most likely not be able to buy the biscuits from your local hardware dealer.

When you get the biscuits home, store them in sealed containers (for example, Ziplock bags), because they are affected by humidity (Illus. 2-3). Store them in as dry a place as possible. Improper storage could be expensive, since the biscuits cost as much as 3 cents apiece. Some biscuits fit very tightly when they are first inserted, and if they are

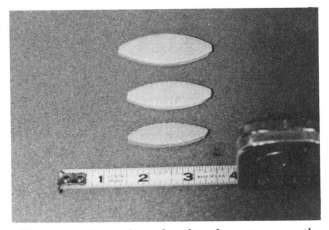

Illus. 2-1.   General woodworking biscuits are available in three basic sizes, as shown here. From top to bottom, they are numbers 20, 10, and 0 biscuits.

11

Illus. 2-2.   A look at some of the commercially available biscuits. On the left are generic biscuits, in the middle are Porter-Cable biscuits, and on the right are Lamello biscuits. At the bottom right is a Lamello #20 clamping biscuit, which is described on page 15. All of these biscuits are very similar, so buy the cheapest ones available.

Illus. 2-3.   Biscuits should be stored in airtight containers.

stored improperly they can swell and become even more difficult to insert.

Biscuit Strength and Effectiveness

Biscuit joints are very strong. Illus. 2-4 and 2-5 show two pieces of maple, each 1 inch thick × 12 inches long, edge-joined with three biscuits. These were scraps from my very cold winter shop. I was impatient to glue the machined pieces when I brought them into my house from the shop and set them on the radiator for nearly an hour—a foolish move. The pieces began to crack or split badly, but I glued them anyway and let the glue dry overnight. Despite the serious checking, some of which appeared to run two-thirds of the way through the boards, I had to hit the pieces with a hammer to break them, and even then it wasn't the joint that broke!

If you use biscuits, you will be virtually guaranteed extremely solid joining work. Noted furniture-maker Graham Blackburn sometimes joins chairs with biscuits. Even load-bearing shelves such as those used for phonograph records can be biscuit-joined in place.

How to Use Biscuits

All joining biscuits are made of solid beech wood. Joining biscuits are made as follows: Felled tree trunks are cut to length and sawn into boards, which are then cut square and dried. Then the material is sawn into laths, which are processed to biscuits on a stamping press before they are sorted, counted, and packed.

Biscuits are used for joining surfaces, corners, and frames, and can be used in joints that are butted, staggered, or mitred. They can be used on chipboard, solid wood, plywood, or other sheet materials.

Biscuits work like splines and dowels as they help to line up adjoining surfaces. However, they are preferred over dowels because they provide a greater wood-to-wood-surface gluing area, although you should provide as many of them as possible since they are the only source of structural integrity.

When using the biscuits, simply do the following: Align your cuts. Since the biscuit slots are cut slightly larger than the biscuits, you don't have to line up your cuts perfectly lengthwise (Illus. 2-6). However, the joiner must be set up square or it may misalign things widthwise. To verify that the joiner is set up square, simply check the joiner by placing an engineer's square (or other small square) against the edge of its face. If the tool is set square, the fence will meet the square all along its length (Illus. 2-7).

Illus. 2-4. *These boards began to check badly after they dried out on a radiator while being warmed for gluing. Note, however, that the biscuits did not fail—a tribute to their strength.*

Illus. 2-5. *To break the biscuit that joined these pieces, I had to put one piece in my bench vise and apply all of my body weight to the other member.*

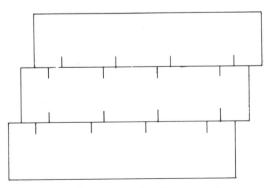

Illus. 2-6. *You have ¼ inch of leeway when you are aligning a pair of joints. This should be enough to allow for perfect alignment.*

Illus. 2-7.   To verify that a joiner is square, place a square against the edge of its face. The fence should meet the square all along its length.

First, cut and properly align the slots. Cut the slots a bit deeper than half of the biscuit's width to accommodate the glue. This also makes them slightly longer than the biscuits, thus allowing nearly a quarter inch of lengthwise play so that you can adjust the pieces to be flush at their ends. Use a knife-like implement such as a chisel to

Illus. 2-8.   Use a knife-like implement to remove the chips from the slots before beginning to assemble the joint.

remove the chips from the slots before beginning assembly (Illus. 2-8). Then glue the slots with polyvinyl acetate (PVA) glue such as Elmer's or Titebond. Glue them carefully. Dropping glue down both sides of the slots (Illus. 2-9) is the best way of gluing except when you are edge-gluing or joining mitres. Just filling the slots can be too messy, and gluing the biscuit directly would dictate assembly times that are impossibly short.

The biscuits will set soon after insertion and expand, thus producing the required lateral (side to side) pressure inside the groove. The continuous setting process of the glue leads to growing mechanical strength, which means that only a very short time is needed for clamping.

While biscuit joining itself is very fast, take your time when cutting the members to be joined. Cut them accurately and plan the assembly of your project carefully. (Cutting techniques are discussed in Chapter 6.) A biscuit-joined project can be assembled much more neatly than any other type. You will find that you use far less glue, so you can all but "finish-sand" the pieces before finally assembling them.

Dealing with Biscuit Pucker

When a biscuit is inserted into ⅜-inch-thick stock, the biscuit sometimes fills the cut so completely that biscuit-shaped protrusions appear on both faces of the stock. If you scrape the glue bead off when gluing an assembly, you may not notice these slight protrusions. However, as the wood adjusts, the protrusions will shrink to leave puckered indentations. Keeping the biscuits at least ¼ inch from any surface is a satisfactory way to prevent this problem.

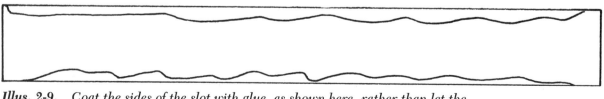

Illus. 2-9.   Coat the sides of the slot with glue, as shown here, rather than let the glue pool in the bottom of the slot.

Illus. 2-10. *A close-up of a size-20 Lamello plastic clamping biscuit. These biscuits are used with wooden biscuits for hard-to-clamp joints. They may prove useful in helping you to complete awkward joining projects.*

Accessory Biscuits

Some manufacturers sell accessory biscuits for use with joiners. Generally, these biscuits can be used more quickly than the wooden ones and frequently produce a very strong joint. The following descriptions of some of the accessories will prove helpful to you.

Lamello Clamping Biscuits

The plastic, toothed, size-20 Lamello clamping biscuits (Illus. 2-10) are expensive. A box of these biscuits, however, should last you a long time. You may not use them often, but when you do, you'll realize how valuable they are. They are used with wooden biscuits on hard-to-clamp joints. They are time-savers on projects that are too awkward in shape to clamp or on projects that are difficult to neatly glue.

Skil Self-Locking Plastic Biscuits

Skil self-locking plastic biscuits (Illus. 2-11) help woodworkers make convenient joints which are glued and force-fit, but not clamped. The immediate advantages are reduced assembly time and joints that aren't affected by humidity. More important, these biscuited joints are essential in places where clamping isn't possible.

I joined two pieces of 14-inch-long maple scrap using one of these biscuits without glue. I couldn't tear the pieces apart freehand, even though I used all my strength. Illus. 2-12 shows how they were separated. I was able to create an opening between the boards with a crowbar and then pry

them apart. To remove the biscuit from the separated joint, I used a chisel with a ⅛-inch-wide blade and a mallet, causing damage to the biscuit, but none to the work (Illus. 2-13). I then reassembled the joint with the same biscuit, and again could not force it apart by hand. If you must disassemble a joint like this, use a narrow chisel rather than a pair of pliers (Illus. 2-14). The pliers will merely destroy the biscuit without removing it.

Much less brittle and expensive than their Lamello counterparts, the Skil self-locking bis-

Illus. 2-11. *A side view of a Skil self-locking biscuit.*

Illus. 2-12. *This joint, assembled with Skil self-locking plastic biscuits, was finally broken with a crowbar.*

Illus. 2-13. *Here a chisel is being used to remove the biscuit from a joint. Note the chips of plastic biscuit forming on the edge.*

Illus. 2-14. *Trying to remove the clamping biscuits with a pair of pliers didn't work at all.*

cuits make permanent joints, especially when used properly with glue. They are an inexpensive solution to many difficult joining problems, and I believe they should be your first choice in clamping biscuits.

Lamello Simplex Knockdown Fittings

Lamello Simplex knockdown fittings (Illus. 2-15) are made of aluminum and are expensive. These fittings are used to assemble or disassemble furniture easily. In the right application, they could be very useful. Sooner or later, we will be buying these fittings for frames, aprons, and for other supports for heavy loads. One can even use them in pairs on a bed frame.

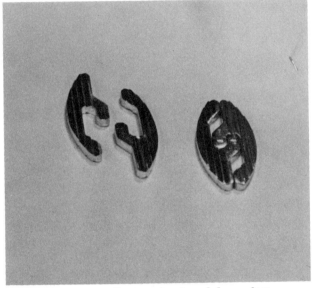

Illus. 2-15.   Lamello Simplex knockdown fittings are made of aluminum. Sold in pairs, they are very helpful on items that must be quickly assembled or taken apart.

As with the other Lamello biscuits mentioned in this chapter, you do not have to use a Lamello biscuit joiner to make the plunge-cut into which the fittings are inserted. Installation is easy: Simply cut mating slots, apply epoxy cement in both slots, and insert a fitting in each slot. Lamello even has an insertion tool, shown in Illus. 2-16, for this job if you want to ensure precisely centered positioning every time. This tool is certainly more of a luxury than a necessity. I have had great success installing these fittings freehand.

Other Lamello Biscuits

Until now, one disadvantage of biscuit joining was that the joints were always too wide for use with face-frame joinery. (A face-frame joint is a joint that attaches the face of furniture to the carcass, or body.) There are now biscuits available which can be used for face-frame joinery. One such biscuit is the Lamello H-9 (Illus. 2-17). These biscuits are only 1½ inches long. Use them with a special cutter that will fit almost any joiner to join picture-frame stock as narrow as 1¼ inches (Illus. 2-18). If you do much framing, this setup is almost a necessity. These biscuits are also less than half the thickness of standard biscuits. If you use many of them, it might be a good idea to mount the H-9 cutting in a separate joiner. Before cutting, be sure to set the depth of cut to its maximum (D on some machines).

Another such biscuit is the Lamello #11 round biscuit (Illus. 2-19). This biscuit is also good for face-frame construction.

Lamello has also introduced spline stock in two other sizes: 13 inches long × 1⁷⁄₁₆ inches wide and 13¾ inches long × 2¹⁄₁₆ inches wide. This stock will be useful for joining material that can be slotted rather than merely biscuited, and it can be cut to the sizes needed (Illus. 2-20). (In this case, slotted stock refers to the dadoes cut to the width of the biscuits.)

Other new biscuits are the #6, which is 3⁵⁄₁₆ inches long by 1³⁄₁₆ inches wide, and the #4, which is 2⁵⁄₈ inches long by 1⅞ inches wide (Illus. 2-17). Both of these biscuits are useful for joining extra-large material. To cut slots for the #6 biscuits, set the depth-of-cut gauge to its maximum, make the first plunge cut, withdraw the machine, move the machine over ⅜ inch, and make another plunge cut. When you lay out the joint (see Chapter 6), mark both plunge points, rather than try to achieve paired plunging by eye. To cut the slots for the #4 biscuit, set the depth-of-cut gauge to cut for S (which is a bit deeper than you'd cut for a #20 biscuit; unfortunately, the S setting is not available on all joiners), make the plunge cut, move the joiner over slightly (⅜ inch will be too far if you want a precise fit), and make another plunge cut. Before cutting slots for either of these

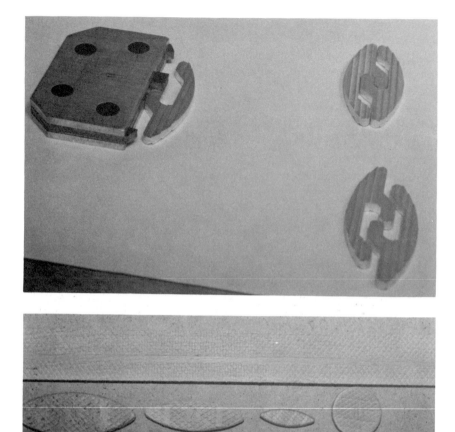

Illus. 2-16.   *A Simplex insertion tool (left) and a pair of inserts.*

Illus. 2-17.   *An assortment of Lamello biscuits. In the top row, from left to right, are the # 6, 4, 9, and 11 biscuits.*

Illus. 2-18.   *A Lamello number 9 biscuit and cutter (left) compared to a standard-sized biscuit and cutter.*

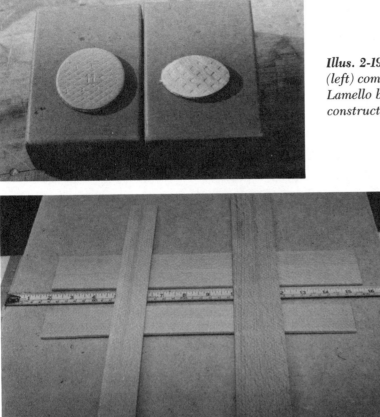

Illus. 2-19.   *The Lamello number 11 round biscuit (left) compared to another "round" biscuit. This Lamello biscuit is excellent for face-frame construction.*

Illus. 2-20.   *Lamello splines above and below a ruler.*

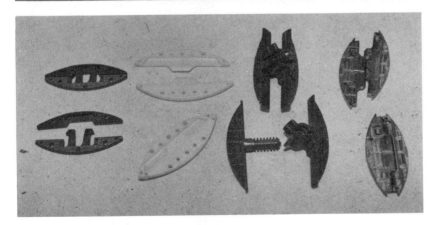

Illus. 2-21.   *Häfele/Knapp knockdown fittings do not have to be glued or clamped in place.*

biscuits, make practice cuts in scrap stock before beginning, especially if you don't want the slots to be so oversize as to be sloppy.

Lamello biscuits can be bought in home centers and through some woodworking catalogues.

Häfele/Knapp Biscuit Fasteners

Häfele/Knapp also sells several types of biscuit fasteners. The advantage of *Häfele/Knapp knockdown fittings* is that they can be used to make permanent joints without time-consuming gluing and clamping (Illus. 2-21). Several of these useful fittings are discussed below.

The *Häfele/Knapp Champ biscuit fasteners* consist of two pieces of precision-engineered rugged plastic (Illus. 2-22 and 2-23). Each piece is

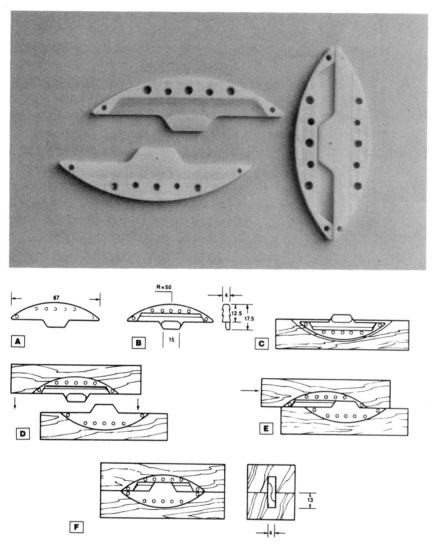

Illus. 2-22. *Häfele/Knapp Champ biscuit fasteners are made of rugged plastic.*

Illus. 2-23. *Views showing how the Häfele/Knapp Champ fastener is used.*

glued into a biscuit groove or slot and, with common joiners, glue-pressed firmly in place with the template provided. You can easily cut the slot or groove with a standard cutter that comes with the joiner using a #10 blade setting. You can also use a groove cutter with a 45-millimetre-diameter, 4-millimetre wide blade.(The groove cutter, also called a slotting cutter, can be a router bit used in a router that is used to cut the biscuit slots.) Once the glue is dried, you can either simply interlock the pieces for a snug, precise fit that can be readily disassembled, or glue the pieces for a perfect and permanent fit. The Champ biscuit fastener tightens automatically as the pieces are pressed together.

The *Häfele/Knapp Metal connector* is an ideal connector for quick, strong, tight joints (Illus. 2-24 and 2-25). Each section of a Häfele/Knapp Metal connector is securely fitted into a 12.6 millimeter-deep biscuit groove and firmly anchored with two screws. The joint holds even heavy loads securely. When needed, the connector has the added advantage of locking the joint in one direction if you bend the flap bolt outward in the desired direction with a screwdriver. For pressed-wood applications, the joint should be secured with glue. (Pressed wood is composed of wood chips that have been glued together.)

The *Häfele/Knapp Quick fastener* (Illus. 2-26 and 2-27) mounts securely with just one hammer blow. You don't need clamps. You don't even have to wait for the glue in the groove to dry. This quick installation makes the Häfele/Knapp Quick fastener the ideal connector for a variety of applications, particularly door frames and other door fittings. Simply cut a groove using a standard biscuit cutter. Apply some common joiner's glue. Then, using the template provided, instantly secure each piece in its respective groove with a hammer. For a permanent, precise joint, apply glue to the gap between the two connector pieces. The joint holds tightly and securely without the need for clamps.

The *Häfele/Knapp Clip fastener* (Illus. 2-28 and 2-29) gives stable connections at 90 degrees for applying mouldings and wooden borders quickly, precisely, and securely. The fastener's unique bolt design makes it readily adjustable for precise alignment, and mouldings or other cabinet and furniture components snap into place firmly. Connections made with these fasteners can be readily disassembled.

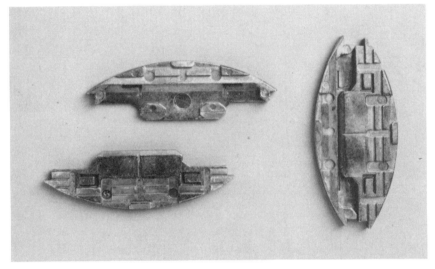

Illus. 2-24. The Häfele/Knapp Metal connector can hold very heavy loads securely.

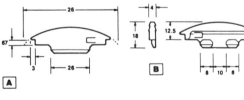
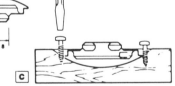
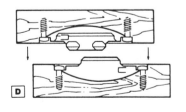
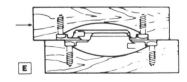
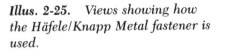

Illus. 2-25. Views showing how the Häfele/Knapp Metal fastener is used.

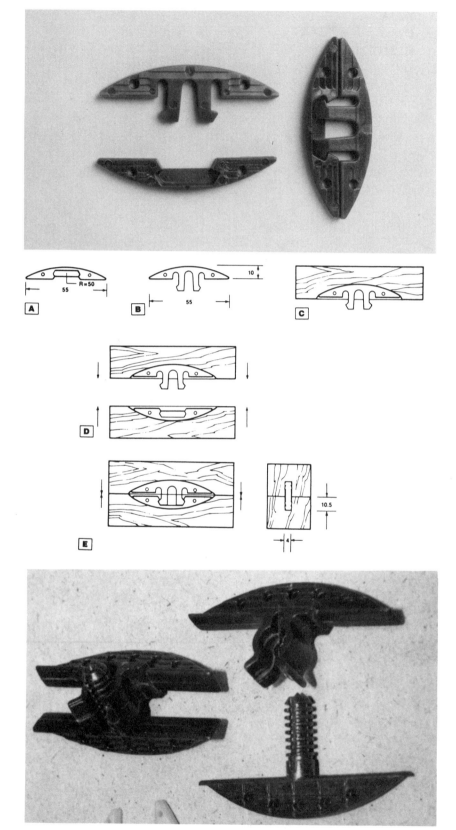

Illus. 2-26. *The Häfele/Knapp Quick fastener can be mounted very speedily.*

Illus. 2-27. *Views showing how the Häfele/Knapp Quick fasteners are used.*

Illus. 2-28. *The Häfele/Knapp Clip fastener allows you to apply mouldings and wooden borders quickly.*

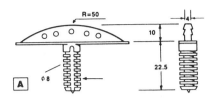

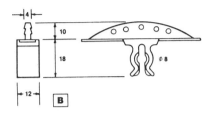

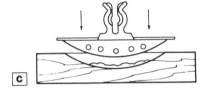

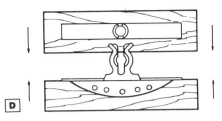

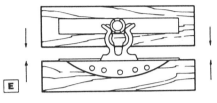

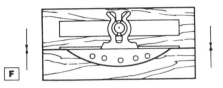

Illus. **2-29.** *Views showing how the Häfele/Knapp Clip fastener is used.*

Chapter 3

SELECTING A BISCUIT JOINER

The machines that cut the biscuit slots have changed considerably over the last ten years (Illus. 3-1). A positive trend in the market today is that there are many more low-to-moderate-priced joiners. A few years ago there were really no alternatives to the high-cost top-of-the-line models. Today, there are a number of machines of equal quality that cost half the price.

In the course of preparing to write *Biscuit Joiner Handbook*, I tested every biscuit joiner available in the United States and a few in other countries, so I have a good idea of the models on the market. The information in this chapter and the chart that appears on pages 38 and 39 describe a few of the many models that will appeal to first-time biscuit-joiner users.

Selection Guidelines

Before buying a biscuit joiner, pay attention to the following guidelines:

1. Don't buy a joiner sight unseen from a catalogue photo or the description of an advertisement. Don't even accept verbatim my descriptions of the models. Operate the joiner or at least examine it firsthand before deciding whether to buy it. When examining a joiner, make sure to check that its base, faceplate, and fence are flat and square to each other. If the surfaces are flat and square, they'll cut accurate joints, and the pieces can be assembled more accurately.

2. Joiners range in price from under $100 to over $700. Buy the best-quality joiner you can

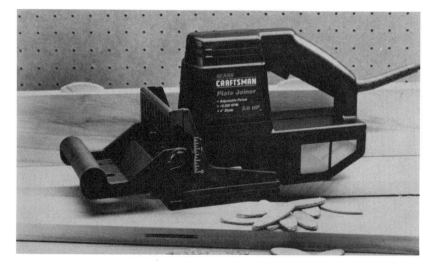

Illus. 3-1. Today's biscuit joiners, also referred to as plate joiners, are generally of higher quality than the joiners that first appeared on the market over 10 years ago, and are much more user-friendly.

afford. The extra money you spend when purchasing the joiner will prove cost-effective in the long run.

3. Check the warranty of the joiner. Some joiners have a full year's limited warranty, and others a six-month warranty.

4. Before shopping around for a biscuit joiner, refer to the chart on pages 38 and 39. This provides information that will help you compare the various ones.

5. When you get the joiner home, write the model number, serial number, and date of purchase on the cover of the manual. Keep your manual with all your other tool manuals. Save all sales receipts, repair records, and other related material with the manual. Keeping your materials organized thus ensures that you'll have them when needed.

6. Pay attention to the variety of accessories joiner manufacturers sell. These accessories should not influence you in deciding what biscuit joiner you buy, but will make that biscuit joiner easier to use.

Lamello Biscuit Joiners

Lamello has been one of the leaders in biscuit-joiner manufacturing. A decade ago I considered its Lamello Top the best joiner on the market. Since then the Lamello Top has been discontinued, superseded by the Lamello Top Ten (Illus. 3-2).

The Lamello Top Ten has many outstanding features. Its angle-adjustment scale offers a fine graduation of numbers. It has a handle that is much more comfortable to use than the old-style D handles (Illus. 3-3), and a front-face height scale that is very easy to read (Illus. 3-4). The joiner is also very durable, as I found out when it accidentally fell off my workbench but was undamaged.

The Lamello Top Ten has a 700-watt, 10,000 rpm (revolutions per minute) motor that can easily cut even the toughest material. It can cut wood up to ¾ inch thick without the need for a flap faceplate. Like its predecessor, the Lamello Top, it is one of the most expensive joiners on the market.

Lamello Dynamic Cordless Biscuit Joiner

The Lamello Dynamic is the first cordless biscuit joiner (Illus. 3-5). It has a two-tooth blade that cuts even very tough material easily. Testing the machine, I cut slots in end grain of some "scrap" cherry until I ran out of scraps big enough to use. Each cut seems fresh and new, and the battery didn't give out or even show signs of weakening as I cut perhaps seven to eight dozen size-20 slots in the cherry end grain.

When I first switched on the Lamello Dynamic, it rose in volume to 91 decibels after about four seconds. This qualifies the tool as one of the quietest joiners on the market, although it didn't sound that quiet to me. As I have recommended

Illus. 3-2. The Lamello Top Ten has an angle-adjustment scale that offers a fine graduation of numbers and a front-face height scale that is very easy to read.

Illus. 3-3. *The Lamello Top Ten has a universal handle that is very comfortable to use, even when you're using the tool rearwards or upside down.*

Illus. 3-4. *A close-up of the front-face height scale on the Lamello Top Ten.*

Illus. 3-5. *The Lamello Dynamic cordless biscuit joiner may well be the tool that introduces the next era of convenience in biscuit joining.*

with every other biscuit joiner, wear your hearing protection. If you don't, you'll eventually miss hearing many more pleasant sounds.

The unit features a paper-chip collection bag, and the tool arrived with a package of five. This is a helpful innovation. After all, what's the point in carefully collecting the dust when we are going to dump it out right in our faces anyway? This way, each individual bag can be disposed of. The adapter that holds the paper bag to the tool can also be snapped into my Lamello Top Ten, and probably into the other Lamello models. This snap-in adapter permits so fluid an air flow that most of the chips are collected.

This tool is basically a cordless version of the Lamello Top Ten. The machine comes standard with a 12-volt, 1.7-amp nickel/cadmium battery, a one-hour charger, and dust-bag filters. A 10-minute charge is available as an option. Although this charge will extend the service life of the battery about threefold, the manufacturer recommends a spare battery pack as the best option for most shops.

Makita 3901 Joiner

The Makita 3901 joiner (Illus. 3-6) is a high-quality, moderately priced joiner. It has a 100-inch-long rubber cord set, and a 5.6-amp, 590-watt motor that runs the blade at 10,000 rpm. A dust bag is standard. The joiner runs at 92 decibels, which makes it among the quietest joiners available, and weighs only 6.2 pounds.

The joiner's castings are precisely machined. This is important, because there is essentially no

Illus. 3-6. *The Makita 3901 joiner has a 5.6-amp, 590-watt motor that runs the blade at 10,000 rpm, a front fence that adjusts easily from 0 to 90 degrees, and lock knobs that are on the inside of the joiner instead of the outside.*

leeway allowed for lateral error in biscuit joining. As the mating slots are aligned, they must be parallel to each other. If the cutter or blade is not running square, the slots will not align properly.

Unlike most other joiners, access to the blade on the Makita joiner is very easy. The holder bolt needs only about two counterclockwise revolutions to release the catch. The bottom panel pivots from the front to reveal the blade. After you've gained access to the blade, a shaft lock helps provide easy blade changes.

The large grip face on the Makita 3901 joiner can be snapped in and out easily for operations where you want the tool to slide, as when cutting slots for splines rather than biscuits. Six cutting depths can be preset by rotating the depth-of-cut adjustment knob; most other mid-priced joiners offer only settings for the #0, 10, and 20 biscuits. The front fence (also referred to as a flap face) adjusts easily from 0 to 90 degrees. Most other mid-priced joiners require a shim of some type to achieve angles other than 0 or 90 degrees. It will save woodworkers a great deal of time.

Makita's lock-downs or position tighteners are on the inside of the joiner rather than on its outside. Thus, on the Makita joiner, unlike other joiners, the center mark for the blade is, in fact, the *actual* center of the tool. This ensures that its lock-downs will not interfere with the work. In addition, its fence runs on a very square rack-and-pinion mechanism that permits precise depth settings with an excellent depth-of-cut scale. When adjusting the mechanism very slightly for square after sliding it onto the machine, you can count on it remaining square through many readjustments.

The Makita joiner has detents at 0, 45, and 90 degrees. (A detent is a positive stop on a biscuit joiner in the form of a series of round holes that have been drilled at various intervals and a device that will drop into place, locking the mechanism.) Also, it has a centerline cast for the blade on its side, something not available on other joiners.

Freud Joiners

When originally introduced a decade ago, the Freud JS 100 was a competent machine, although it did receive some not-so-favorable reviews. The new version, the JS 100A (Illus. 3-7), has many improvements over the older model. It is much quieter than the old version. There is also a more expensive JS 102 joiner, which has more features. Both feature a six-position depth stop instead of the old-style three-position stop. Each stop is an accurate positive stop. More effective bumpers have replaced the old-style positioning pins. In fact, the only difference between the 100A and the 102 is that the 102 has an aluminum flap face (Illus. 3-8).

The Freud joiners have accurately machined castings. They also have an industrial-quality

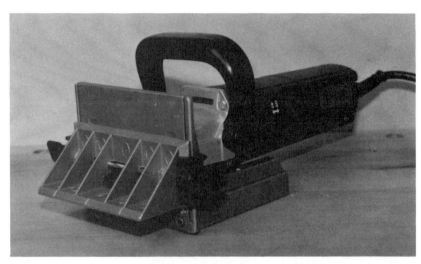

Illus. 3-7.   The Freud JS 100A has a six-position depth stop and a motor that runs at 5 amps and cuts at 10,000 rpm.

Illus. 3-8.   The Freud JS 102 joiner has all of the features of the JS 100A as well as an aluminum flap face.

3¹⁵⁄₁₆-inch-diameter × ⁵⁄₃₂-inch-thick blade with an antikickback design. Their standard dust bag is connected to a large (¹⁵⁄₁₆-inch) orifice at an angle of about 30 degrees, which makes it less likely to clog than the dust bags on many of the competing machines. The Freud joiners have a standard D-handle. Were I going to use this tool full-time, and there are many features that make it an excellent choice for woodworkers, I would seriously consider substituting the Lamello replacement handle for its handle. (See Illus. 3-3 on page 26.)

The 102's 90-degree accessory fence rides the flap snugly. It is accurately cast, so it can be easily mounted. I used one hand to position it, and the other to tighten it. Its motor housing seems large,

but not uncomfortably so in my hands. Test it if you are considering buying the joiner.

Both Freud joiners have a motor that runs at 5 amps and cuts at 10,000 rpm. At 6.2 pounds, they are one of the lighter units, but still feel quite substantial.

Bosch 1650 Joiner

The Bosch 1650 joiner (Illus. 3-9) is a mid-priced joiner with a 5.8-amp, 700-watt motor that cuts at 11,000 rpm. The joiner weighs 10 pounds. Standard equipment includes a dust bag, a blade, a case, a glue bottle, and 20 biscuits. Only the dust hose is optional.

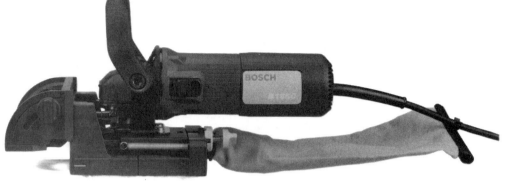

Illus. 3-9. The Bosch 1650 joiner has a 5.8-amp, 700-watt motor that cuts at 11,000 rpm, a well-positioned on/off switch, and three depth-of-cut positions.

Illus. 3-10. A piece of hose clamp attaches the Bosch AirSweep dust-collection system to my Lamello Top Ten, saving a considerable amount of money on the price of dust collection.

The joiner's operating handle is far more comfortable for right- and left-hand operators than the standard D-handle on most joiners. The dust-bag connector is a perfect fit for the Bosch AirSweep dust-collection system, and I strongly recommend buying the hose for use with whatever joiner you choose (Illus. 3-10). The cord set is of typical high Bosch quality. The switch is well positioned for right-hand users, and not as awkward for left-handers as most. Whereas I have no doubts at all about the quality of the grinder motor, the joiner mechanism itself is made of fibreglass-reinforced plastic, which is not my material of choice for hand or power tools. The Bosch 1650 joiner offers only the 0-10-20 depth-of-cut positions rather than the six positions of the top-line joiners, but its setup system makes fine adjustment for precise fits for the three standard sizes of biscuits far easier than it is on most other joiners. A very well designed flap face gives an easy, true vertical adjustment, and correctly cuts mitres from the outside. The machine has accurate scales on its front, and precise centerlines on its front, sides, and bottom. Unfortunately, there are many loose pieces when the flap-face plate is removed.

The blade on the Bosch 1650 joiner has four teeth, in contrast to the six found on most machines, or the 12 offered on some of the more sophisticated machines. The machine recorded a respectable noise level of 94 decibels when tested at arm's length.

PrinceCraft
Jointmatic Joiner

The PrinceCraft Jointmatic 550 joiner (Illus. 3-11) is a Taiwan-made tool which has a Börg label. Its cord is very light and far too short. If I were to use the machine regularly in my shop, I would seriously consider replacing the entire cord set. You can easily gain access to the joiner's blade and insides by removing two knurled nuts and the cover.

There are two scales on the front of the Jointmatic's fence, but they each have English on one side and metric on the other, rather than a pair of combination scales that might help to ensure a more accurate setup. The joiner does have an accurate single scale on the user side of the fence. On the side of the machine is a line which marks the *top* of the blade rather than its center. It would be better if it were centered.

The push pins on the joiner can be adjusted in and out from the outside of the tool. This seems to be an obsolete feature, and the rubber push pads found on other joiners grip the work better. The joiner's six-position depth-of-cut scale has a positive feel without being too tight. Similarly, detents mark the important angles on the flap-face scale. Unlike any of the other joiners, the Jointmatic's flap face can be tilted past 90 degrees.

Unlike virtually all of the other joiners, the Jointmatic has a pair of tie-down holes on either side which can be used to mount the joiner to a bench.

Sears Craftsman
17501 Biscuit Joiner

The Sears Craftsman model 17501 biscuit joiner (Illus. 3-12) is probably the least expensive joiner on the market. Although most of the tool is made of plastic, the adjusting mechanism is made of metal. It has some very helpful features. These include a large, nonslip pad which covers the entire faceplate. The fibreglass-loaded nylon fence has a comfortable handle. The sturdy 10-foot cord is longer than cords on almost all other joiners. At arm's length, the joiner's 6-amp, ⅝-horsepower, 10,000 rpm motor runs at only 93 decibels, even when cutting into rock-maple end grain. (End grain is the porous ends of the wood fibre on the board.)

The Sears 17501 joiner includes a standard dust-collection basket that is extremely convenient to use (Illus. 3-13). One "drawback" is that the basket has to be emptied regularly. The joiner's front fence is clearly marked with depth- and bevel-adjusting angles, and, while the joiner can be set to cut at any angle up to 90 degrees, there are positive detent stops at 15-degree intervals.

There are lines on the sides, top, and bottom of

Illus. 3-11.   The Börg Jointmatic 550 joiner has a six-position depth-of-cut scale, a flap fence that can be tilted past 90 degrees, and tie-down holes on either side which can be used to mount the joiner to a bench.

Illus. 3-12.   Some of the features on the Sears Craftsman 17501 joiner include a 6-amp, ⅝-horsepower motor that runs at 10,000, a large, nonslip pad which covers the entire faceplate, and a standard dust-collection basket.

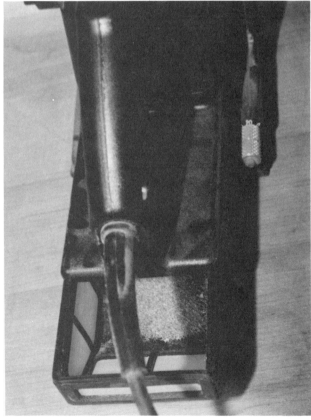

Illus. 3-13.   A close-up of the dust-collection basket on the Sears 17501 joiner. This basket is very handy, but fills up quite quickly.

the joiner that indicate the location of the cut. The carton it is sold in has information on cutting mitre, edge-to-edge, and table leg and apron joints.

Virutex AB II Joiner

The Spanish-made Virutex AB 11 joiner (Illus. 3-14) is made of heavy-grade aluminum and has a 550-watt motor that runs at 10,000 rpm. It comes with a standard dust pickup adapter that is very easy to use. The adapter simply slides into a channel on the side of the joiner (Illus. 3-15).

If you were to look at the machine from the front, you would note that the knob on the right of the machine adjusts the flap face. It is a large, easy-to-adjust knob. The faceplate has both inch and millimetre designations on its scales.

Porter-Cable 555 Joiner

The Porter-Cable 555 joiner (Illus. 3-16), the first American-made entry in the joiner market, has several features that make it unique. Its 5-amp, 8,000 rpm motor drives its blades by belt rather than by helical gear (Illus. 3-17). The belt is quiet and also very strong, although it might be a good idea to have an extra belt on hand.

Because of its radical design, the Porter-Cable 555 is not only one of the most comfortable of the joiners to operate, but at just under five pounds it is also the lightest. This lightness allows you to operate the tool all day, and makes the joiner a

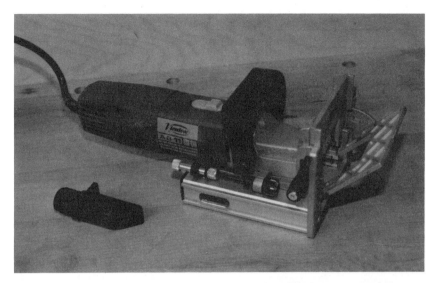

Illus. 3-14. Some of the features on the Virutex AB11 joiner include a 550-watt motor that runs at 10,000 rpm, a large, easy-to-use flap-face adjustment knob, and a dust pickup adapter that simply slides into a channel on the side of the joiner.

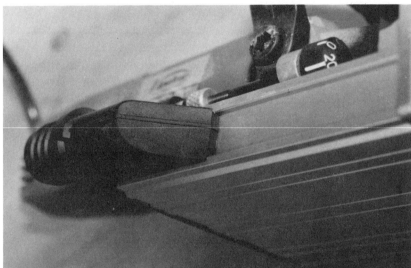

Illus. 3-15. A close-up of the Virutex dust-hose fitting, which slides into the extrusion.

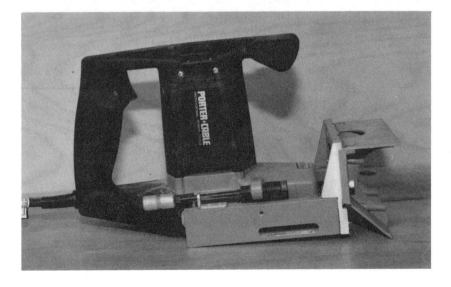

Illus. 3-16. The Porter-Cable 555 joiner has an unusual design in that its 5-amp, 8,000 rpm motor drives its blades by belt rather than by helical gear.

Illus. 3-17.   The drive belt on the Porter-Cable 555 joiner is unique among the joiners. It is quiet and very strong.

very safe joiner to use because it reduces stress on the operator.

The Porter-Cable 555 joiner is different from the other joiners in that it indexes for mitre cuts against the *outside* of the work rather than the inside. This is what causes the Porter-Cable joiner to look radically different from the others. Illus. 3-18 shows the unusual faceplate. Illus. 3-19 shows the underside of the joiner.

Black & Decker Joiners

Black & Decker, Elu, and DeWalt joiners (Illus. 3-20–3-24) all come from Black & Decker. They are the same machine with different-colored housings. The machines are quiet and very accurate. The trigger on each of them is on the underside of the joiner's base; I find it difficult to operate the trigger because of an old hand injury. The tool's rack-and-pinion adjustment and dust-collection bag are of good quality.

Skil 1605 Joiner

The Skil joiner is a low-cost tool with a motor that runs at 5.5 amps and cuts at 12,000 rpm (Illus. 3-24). This is the type of joiner that the average woodworker will be able to buy off the shelf in his neighborhood home center. Most of the other joiners appear to be bought through a professional tool dealer or through mail order.

The Skil joiner is made of fibre-reinforced acrylic, which gives strength and makes the joiner inexpensive. It has a depth-adjustment dial that can be set to cut #0, 10, and 20 biscuits. It has

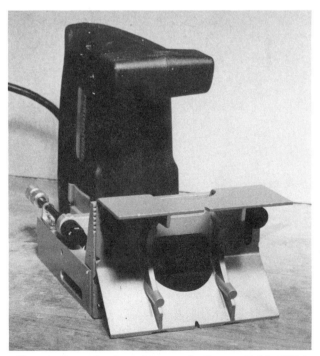

Illus. 3-18.   The faceplate on the Porter-Cable 555 is different from the faceplates on other joiners.

Illus. 3-19.   *A close-up of the underside of the Porter-Cable 555. Note the long layout line that extends right up its middle.*

Illus. 3-20–3-24.   *A look at some of the joiners available from Black & Decker.*

Illus. 3-21.

Illus. 3-22.

Illus. 3-23.

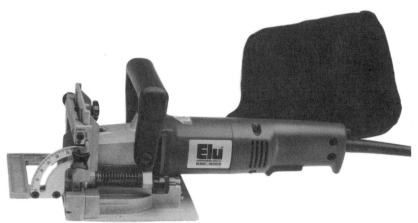

Illus. 3-24.

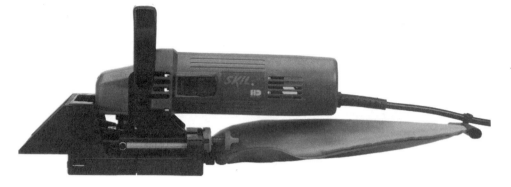

Illus. 3-25.   The Skil joiner is made of fibre-reinforced acrylic, has a depth-adjustment setting for #0, 10, and 20 biscuits, and has rubber feet that prevent the machine from skidding across the work.

rubber feet that prevent the machine from skidding across the work. A vacuum adapter can be added for dust collection. An accessory flap-front fence is available. A dust bag is permanently mounted to the tool. This inexpensive joiner is sure to be popular with many woodworkers.

Ryobi JM-80K Joiner

The Ryobi JM-80K joiner has a 120-volt, 6-amp motor that spins its 8-tooth blade at 10,000 rpm (Illus. 3-26 and 3-27). Easily adjustable for standard #0, 10, and 20 biscuits, this 6½-pound tool

sports a 10-foot cord and a standard dust bag. Unlike some of the other joiners, this one has a plastic body with a metal fence that is adjustable from 0 to 135 degrees, with positive stops at every 45 degrees. Stiff springs prevent you from cutting a slot "accidentally" in a spot where you don't want one. This tool, at 92 decibels, is quieter than many of the other joiners.

The Ryobi JM-80K joiner has a rubber face like that of some of the other joiners featured in this chapter. This rubber face will keep the tool still while you are cutting slots with it. The joiner sells for approximately $100, which makes it one of the least expensive joiners on the market.

Illus. 3-26.   The Ryobi JM-80k joiner features a rubber face that prevents the tool from moving while you cut slots with it, a plastic body with a metal fence that is adjustable from 0 to 135 degrees, and an 8-tooth blade that revolves at 10,000 rpm.

Illus. 3-27.   The Ryobi JM-80K joiner is one of the best joiners you can buy in the $100 price range. Even the tool's case is extraordinary.

Biscuits and Glue Bottles

Once you have your biscuit joiner, you must secure two other items: biscuits and a glue bottle. Most of the joiners come with a few biscuits to get you started, but there aren't nearly enough to do even a single project. You will have to buy additional packages. Some vendors sell biscuits in packages of 250 or less rather than in the packages of 1,000 that have been standard for years. The package of 1,000 biscuits costs around $30, although some vendors are now selling them for around $20.

It is important that you have a glue bottle with which to glue the slots. Lamello sells a very good glue bottle. Its tip is made of milled metal, and the bottle comes in a weighted base (Illus. 3-28 and 3-29). It also sells a less expensive model with a plastic tip and a base that you'll have to mount yourself.

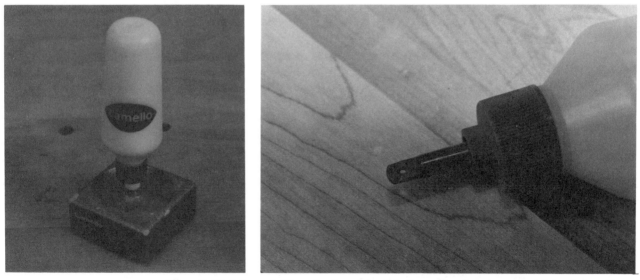

Illus. 3-28 (above left).   A gluer like this Lamello gluer is essential to gluing the slots for the biscuits. Illus. 3-29 (above right). A close-up look at the Lamello gluer at work. It quickly applies the glue to the sides of the slots through channels.

Maker or Distributor	Model	Retail Price (dollars)	Weight (pounds)	Speed (RPM)	Power Consumption (AMPs)	Noise Level (Decibels)
Black & Decker/ DeWalt/Elu (800-923-8665)	Black & Decker 3382	230	6¼	10,000	6.5	94
	DeWalt DW 682	222	6¼	10,000	6.5	94
	Elu 3379	229	6¼	10,000	6.5	94
Fortune Extendables PrinceCraft/Börg/ Jointmatic	Jointmatic 550	120	7½	10,000	6	96
Freud	JS 100A	134	7	10,000	5	92
	JS 102	188	6⅞	10,000	5	92
Lamello Colonial Saw (800-252-6355)	Top Ten	538	7¼	10,000	6.4	92
	Standard Ten	399	7⅛	10,000	5.8	93
	Cobra	250	6⅞	10,000	2.1	94
	Dynamic (cordless)	675–725		24,000 12-volt battery & motor		91
Makita	Makita 3901		6⅕	10,000	5.6	92
Porter-Cable (800-487-8665)	555	159	6½	8,000	5	93
	556	172	6½	8,000	5	93
Ryobi (800-525-2579)	JM-80K	100	6½	10,000	6	96
	JM-100K	209	7¼	9,000	5.3	96
S-B Power Tools (312-286-7330)	Bosch B 1650	158	6	11,000	5.8	94
	Skil HD 1605	123	6	12,000	6	96
Sears	Craftsman 17501	100	6	10,000	6	93
	Bis Kit	39	Specifications depend on your router's specifications			
Virutex (800-847-8839)	AB 11C	250	6⅛	10,000	6	94

Table 3-1.   This table contains information on the features of the biscuit joiners described in this chapter, as well as discontinued models and models not discussed. Comparing the features of the different models will give you a good idea of what is available on the market.

Table 3-1 continued.

Maker or Distributor	Model	Dust-Collection Features	Anti-Slip Features	Angle-Cutting Capabilities	Non-Standard Size Biscuits that can be used
Black & Decker/ DeWalt/Elu	Black & Decker 3382	bag/vacuum	rubber dots	variable	M
	DeWalt DW 682	bag/vacuum	rubber dots	variable	M
	Elu 3379	bag/vacuum	rubber dots	variable	M
Fortune Extendables PrinceCraft/Börg/ Jointmatic	Jointmatic 550	bag	pins	variable	S/D/M
Freud	JS 100A	bag	rubber dots	45°/90°	S/D/M
	JS 102	bag	rubber dots	variable	S/D/M
Lamello Colonial Saw	Top Ten	vacuum	rubber dots	variable	S/D/M
	Standard Ten	vacuum	rubber dots	45°/90°	S/D/M
	Cobra	vacuum	rubber dots	45°/90°	S/D/M
	Dynamic (cordless)	bag/vacuum	rubber dots	variable	S/D/M
Makita	Makita 3901	bag/vacuum	rubber face	variable	S/D/M
Porter-Cable	555	none	pins	45°/90°	none
	556	none	pins	variable	none
Ryobi	JM-80K	bag	rubber face	variable	none
	JM-100K	bag	rubber face	variable	none
S-B Power Tools	Bosch B 1650	bag/vacuum	rubber dots	variable	none
	Skil HD 1605	bag	none	45°/90°	none
Sears	Craftsman 17501	box	rubber face	45°/90°	none
	Bis Kit	Specifications depend on your router's specifications			
Virutex	AB 11C	vacuum	rubber dots	variable	S/D/M

Chapter 4

SAFETY TECHNIQUES AND GENERAL CUTTING GUIDELINES

Safety Instructions

Although the biscuit joiner is one of the safest tools in the workshop, any woodworking done with a joiner or any other power tool remains a potentially dangerous activity. Cutters are sharp, and high-power motors move them at very high speeds. I've seen far more accidents caused by operator error than equipment failure during my years of woodworking. Most of the accidents occur because the operator is either careless or in a hurry.

The following rules will help to minimize operator error in your shop, thus ensuring a safer working environment.

1. Before using your joiner (or any other tool), read and understand its operations manual. A good manual will describe techniques and procedures that will help to keep you safe.

2. Keep the cutters sharp and maintain them properly. (See the next chapter for information on how to do this.) Dull tools force you to exert extra pressure when you cut. This makes you more

likely to slip and, thereby, get your hands in the way of the cutting edge. A good rule is to sharpen your joiner's blade when it *starts* to feel dull rather than wait until you're sure that it is dull.

3. Clamp your work to a bench so that you can use both hands to guide the tool. I have seen many woodworkers holding a piece in one hand while operating a joiner with the other. Do *not* do this! It is very dangerous, particularly when you are working with small pieces.

4. Use the D-handle on your joiner (Illus. 4-1). It is part of the joiner's safety equipment. In this book, you'll see many photos of the joiner being held by the motor housing for a one-handed operation. To ensure your complete safety, hold the tool by the motor housing *and* by the D-handle. If this accomplishes nothing else, it ensures that you won't be holding a piece so small that the biscuit joiner's blade will go through it when you make a plunge cut.

5. Wear the proper safety equipment when woodworking (Illus. 4-2). Always wear safety glasses or goggles. When using a tool that throws lots of chips, wear a face shield as well. When

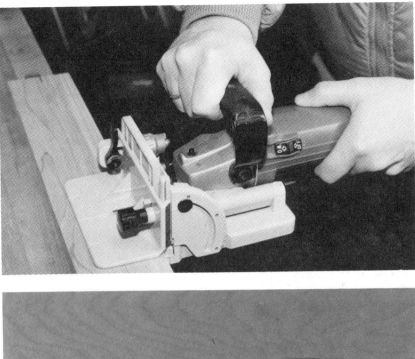

Illus. 4-1. To ensure your complete safety when using the biscuit joiner, hold it with one hand by its motor housing, and by its D-handle with your other hand.

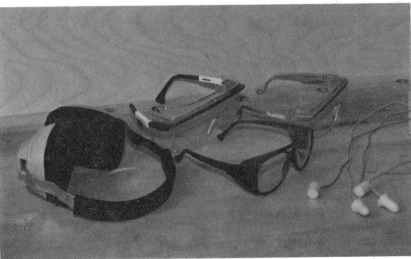

Illus. 4-2. Safety glasses or goggles should be part of the safety equipment you wear when using a biscuit joiner.

using a tool as loud as a joiner, wear hearing protection. Wear a dust mask whenever you're sanding or doing operations that produce lots of dust. If there is a dust collector available for a tool, *use it every time you switch on the tool* (Illus. 4-3).

6. Wear steel-tipped shoes when you are working. Don't wear loose clothing. Roll up your sleeves. If you have long hair, tie it back. Anything loose can be pulled into a cutter if it gets caught. Don't wear jewelry, not even a wedding ring.

7. Never attempt to adjust a biscuit joiner or any power tool while it is plugged in or has its battery in place.

8. Do not do any woodworking if you have taken drugs or alcohol. Even over-the-counter and prescription drugs can cause drowsiness and other effects that would make it dangerous to use woodworking tools, so read the labels and follow your doctor's advice.

9. Most important, pay attention to what you're doing. Let your good sense be your guide. Think through each procedure before you do it. If you *feel* a procedure presents a safety hazard, find an alternative way to accomplish the same result.

Remember, it's important to think about safety on a regular, habitual basis. Only your constant

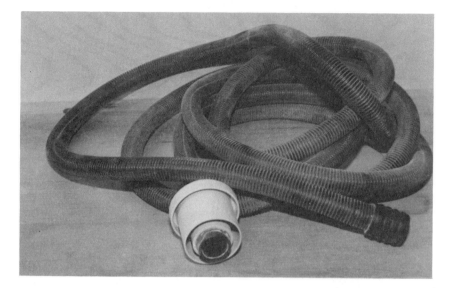

Illus. 4-3.   Use a dust-collection system such as this Bosch Air-Stream dust hose when using a biscuit joiner.

vigilance will protect you from injury in the woodworking shop.

Biscuit-Joining Guidelines

Observe the following biscuit-joining guidelines to ensure that you make accurate biscuit joints:

1. Measure twice and cut once. Always double-check your measurements.

2. Mark joint locations clearly. However, mark your layouts lighter than they are shown in this book, in which they serve the additional purpose of making the layout visible in the photographs. In my usual furniture fabrication, the layout marks are very light.

3. Remember that the more biscuits you use, the stronger the joint will be. Biscuits are preferable to dowels since they provide a greater wood-to-wood-surface gluing area, but you should use as many of them as possible since they are the only source of structural integrity.

4. Clamp the matching joints very square to one another.

5. Cut the slots a bit deeper than half of the biscuits' width to accommodate the glue. This also makes them slightly longer than the biscuits, thus allowing nearly a quarter inch of lengthwise play so that you can adjust the pieces to make them flush at their ends.

6. Test-fit the piece with dry biscuits before gluing.

7. Glue carefully. For the most part, gluing inside the biscuit slots is usually sufficient, except when you are using biscuit joints to align boards for edge-gluing. Use a glue bottle if possible. It will get the glue onto the sides rather than the bottom of the slots, which is what is needed. Light squeeze-out is acceptable, even desirable. Get rid of the squeeze-out early in the process by wiping it away. Clamp at fairly close intervals, that is, at intervals of 10–15 inches. You don't have to leave the clamps in place more than about 20–30 minutes. The biscuits will swell and lock the joint long before the glue is dry.

8. Pay attention to the wide range of accessories for biscuit joining available from different manufacturers through catalogues and home centers. These devices will help to make your biscuit joining easier and more pleasant.

Chapter 5

MAINTENANCE TECHNIQUES

Many of us woodworkers are incredibly lax about periodic maintenance of our tools and equipment. Following a regular maintenance schedule is not just a question of keeping expensive tools working, thus preserving our investment in them, but also a matter of safety. Properly lubricated sharp tools are safer than dull ones, because they don't have to be forced into the work.

What is a regular maintenance schedule? The intervals between these maintenance runs depend on the amount of use, the cleanliness of the workshop, the kind of material being worked, etc., but the best advice is to follow the manufacturer's recommendations. Another general guideline is that if the tool looks dirty, clean it.

Unless you are certain that you can put your joiner back together without making serious mistakes, *don't* take it apart. It is surely less expensive to pay an authorized service center to do routine maintenance than to have to pay them to fix a tool that you reassembled improperly.

Check your tool's warranty. If the warranty is still good, return the tool to your dealer or factory-authorized service center rather than opening it yourself. Attempting to repair the tool on your own, even opening its outer assembly, will almost certainly void the warranty, and this could be more expensive than minor repairs.

All biscuit-joiner manufacturers specify that at the very least the second change of brushes

Illus. 5-1. *When disassembling a plunge-type joiner, the first thing you must do is remove the springs with the hook provided.*

(which is the third *set* of brushes) should be done at a factory-authorized service center along with the thorough cleaning and replacement of all gear grease. Let the trained technicians at these centers disassemble the tool when the brushes have to be changed. If you live in or near a major city, such a repair can very likely be done for little more than the cost of the parts—often on a "while you wait" basis.

That said, there may still be times when you have to change the blade and motor brushes yourself, so you should be familiar with blade-changing techniques. To change the blade, do the following: First, remove the blade's cover. On most units it is a simple matter of removing a couple of screws or knurled nuts. On plunge-type joiners, you must remove the springs with the hook provided (Illus. 5-1) and perhaps the depth-of-cut nuts. After they are off, remove the faceplate from the slide assembly by removing the four screws that attach it with a (Phillips) screwdriver (Illus. 5-2–5-4). Be sure to keep any stabilizer pins and their pressure springs in a safe place. Very likely, your *new* joiner will have rubber bumpers instead, and they should require no special attention at all.

At this point, just slide the cover off, leaving the blade exposed. Remove the blade with wrenches or the allen wrenches and spanner provided (Illus. 5-5 and 5-6). On units with a spindle lock, you'll need only one wrench. The blade on any joiner is removed by turning it counterclockwise.

While the blade should require sharpening only approximately every several boxes of biscuits, this disassembly should be done fairly regularly for other reasons, like cleaning, oiling, and other fine-tuning.

Disassembly Steps

If you have to disassemble the tool, pay particular attention to how the parts fit together. The tool's parts list in the manual is not sufficient to ensure proper reassembly. Here are the basic steps to disassembling the tool:

1. Lay out the parts in the order that you take them off the tool (Illus. 5-7).

Illus. 5-2.   *The next step involved in disassembling a joiner is removing the depth-of-cut nuts if needed. Then remove the four nuts that attach the faceplate to the slide assembly, as shown here and in Illus. 5-3 and 5-4.*

Illus. 5-3.   *Removing the nuts that attach the faceplate.*

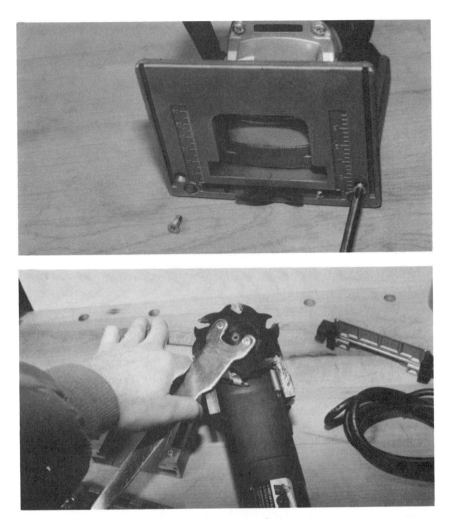

Illus. 5-4. *Removing the nuts that attach the faceplate.*

Illus. 5-5 and 5-6. *Remove the blades with either two wrenches, as shown here and in Illus. 5-6, or with a spindle lock button.*

Illus. 5-6.

2. Remember how tightly each part is fastened so that you can return all the parts to the same torque. (Torque is the force that produces rotation or tension.) Where possible, use an appropriate torque wrench for this work; if, like myself, you don't have one, be sure you remember how much power you used to turn the wrench if you want the part to be reattached only just as tight as it was before you removed it.

3. Handle the fasteners on biscuit joiners with care. Most of them are of metric sizes, and are harder to replace than inch-size fasteners. Use metric nut drivers and wrenches where needed; if you strip the shoulders off the hexagonal nuts, you will make it much more likely that the next time you try to disassemble the joiner you will have a great deal of trouble.

Illus. 5-7. When disassembling a joiner, lay out the parts in the order you take them off the tool.

Illus. 5-8. When reassembling the joiner, make sure that the parts of the joiner are tight and square to each other—not like this!

4. When reassembling the joiner, make sure its parts are assembled tight and square to each other (Illus. 5-8).

Cleaning Joiners

No matter what you disassembled the joiner for, before reassembling it, clean dust and debris from its insides. In fact, blow out the joiner with compressed air (Illus. 5-9–5-11) whenever you see that the joiner has some chips that might block its use. Blow out the motor housing and the blade-guard area. Be sure to wear safety glasses while cleaning with compressed air.

From the slide assembly, remove all traces of the residue formed by the mixing of sawdust and lubricating oil. Use toothpicks or a scratch awl to remove small specs of this residue that are likely to accumulate in the corners. As you replace the slide assembly on the tool, lightly lubricate it (Illus. 5-12). This lubrication should be repeated whenever the slide is not working as smoothly as possible, but not so often that the oil clutters up the work surfaces. Over the past few years, I've become convinced that the bottle of oil that comes with the joiner should last the lifetime of the tool.

Changing Motor Brushes

Motor brushes on the machines are all changed the same way. All manufacturers claim that the tool will simply stop before the tool's armature is destroyed by the carbon brush's spring. Ideally, this is so, but if the joiner is not maintained properly it is possible that the tool's armature will be destroyed. Therefore, after approximately every 50 hours of use, remove the motor cover, generally held in place by just one or two screws, and inspect the brushes. This should not take more than a minute because the brush holders on all machines are easily accessible once the cover is off (Illus. 5-13 and 5-14). Pay attention to the manufacturer's warnings and replace the brushes only with identical parts. To ensure optimum motor life, replace motor brushes in pairs.

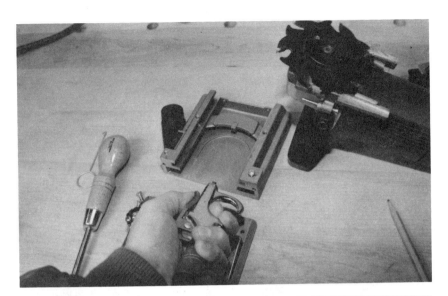

Illus. 5-9–5-11.   Use compressed air to blow out the areas of the joiner shown here and in Illus. 5-10 and 5-11.

Illus. 5-10.

Illus. 5-11.

While you have the motor cover off, it is a good idea to blow the accumulated dust out of the motor; if you don't have a compressor, a can of relatively inexpensive "photographer's air" would be a wise investment (Illus. 5-15 and 5-16). One real advantage to "photographer's air" is that it never contains any liquid like that which sometimes accumulates in compressed-air lines.

Troubleshooting Tips

Following are some of the problems you may have to deal with when using a joiner:

1. **Cord Damage.** Cord damage is almost inevitable in most shops. Replacing the cord shouldn't

Illus. 5-12.   Lubricate the slide assembly on the joiner occasionally, but remember that the bottle of lubricant that comes with the joiner should last the lifetime of the joiner.

Illus. 5-13 and 5-14.   Sometimes you have to use a pair of needlenose pliers to remove tight motor brushes.

Illus. 5-14.

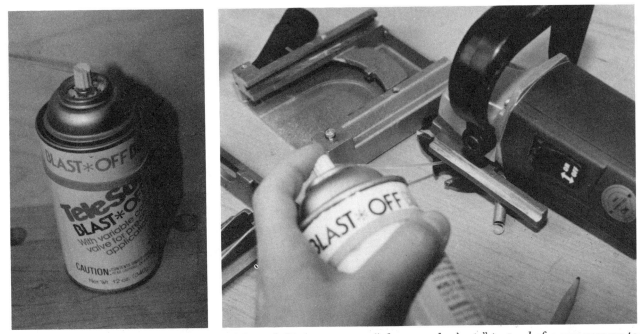

Illus. 5-15 (above left). You can use "photographer's air" instead of a compressor to occasionally remove dust from a motor. Illus. 5-16 (above right). Removing dust from a joiner.

be difficult. Remove the cover and attach an identical cord. To do this, remove the housing. Then, with a screwdriver, loosen the connections on the existing cord, so you can remove it. After you have removed it, slide the new cord through the strain relief and fasten it to the terminals from which you just removed the old one.

2. **Clogged Dust Chute.** A clogged dust chute is invariably the result of infrequent dust removal. After you stop the machine and unplug it, clean the dust chute by probing it with the unit's spring removal hook. Also, never run a joiner with a chip extractor without also running the vacuum cleaner; it only takes a few chips to jam the hose,

and cleaning it will be a major challenge.

3. **A "Skittish" Joiner.** If you find that your unit is "skittish" when you cut very hard material, check your blade for sharpness and review your operating methods. Perhaps you should hold the tool more firmly.

4. **Dropped Joiner.** If you have dropped the tool, check the slide assembly carefully to ascertain that it hasn't been bent out of shape.

Attending regularly to proper maintenance and storage is extremely important. Clean, sharp tools are safe, economical tools.

Chapter 6

LAYING OUT THE WORK

Laying or marking out your work accurately is the key to making accurate biscuit joints. The layout process (also called marking out) consists of making pencil marks on the board where the biscuit and slot cut will meet. First, the mating pieces are cut out. Then the layout marks for the biscuit and slot cut are made. The indicator lines on the front of the joiner's fence and on the front of its base plate (Illus. 6-1–6-3) are used to align and position the lines drawn on the mating pieces of wood.

Biscuit joints can be made much more quickly than dowels or dovetails. Part of the reason for this is that their layout is quicker.

When joining edges of boards or perpendicular surfaces, pencil in lines 2 inches from each end and 4 to 6 inches on center in between (nearly twice that far if edge-joining), as shown in Illus. 6-4. Initially use a combination square to make this layout (Illus. 6-5 and 6-6). After approximately

an hour of such work, you'll be able to make this layout by hand (Illus. 6-7 and 6-8). Make parallel rows (one or more joints from each side) if the workpieces are 1 inch thick or thicker (Illus. 6-9).

Mark the joints so you don't cut them off in the middle of the joint. Since you can use them for alignment only, this is not an issue of strength, but of aesthetics.

When laying out an interior joint, such as on a drawer frame or shelf, make the marks to one side of the member rather than to its center (Illus. 6-10). The pieces must be laid out logically. Since you will be marking the sides of the joints (at the top or bottom, and their front or back), use the *same* side all the time. Be sure to label where the pieces go; if you don't, you may forget the assembly order, and, sooner or later, that will lead to errors that in turn will lead to assemblies that are not square.

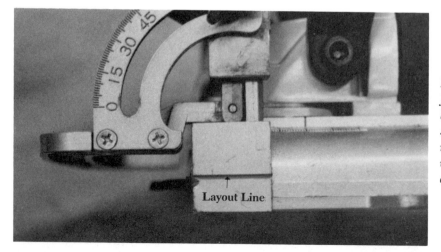

Illus. 6-1. *A side view of the Börg Jointmatic biscuit joiner shows its layout lines, which are used to position the joiner on the lines marked on the mating pieces of wood. All biscuit joiners have layout lines.*

Illus. 6-2. *This view of the Börg Jointmatic biscuit joiner shows the center and side lines on its base-plate. These lines are also used to align the joiner with the marks on the wood, and indicate the potential width and length of the cut.*

Illus. 6-3. *A close-up of a Freud joiner showing its top centerlines.*

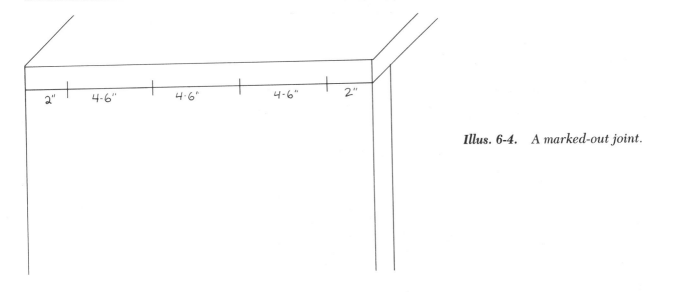

Illus. 6-4. *A marked-out joint.*

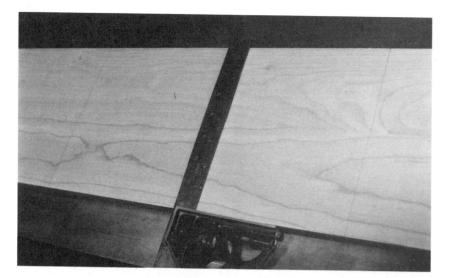

Illus. 6-5 and 6-6. *Laying out the joint with a combination square.*

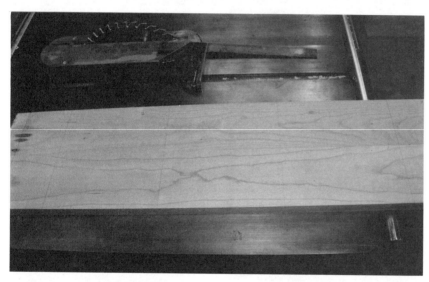

Illus. 6-6.

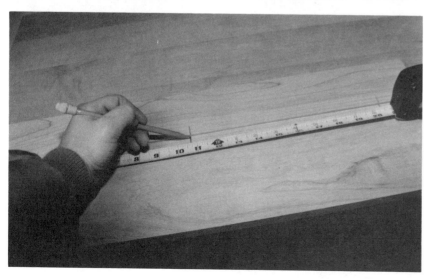

Illus. 6-7. *With some practice you'll be able to lay out the marks without having to use a combination square.*

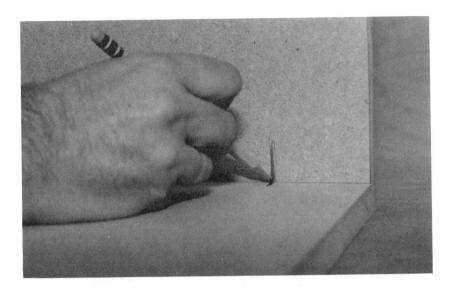

Illus. 6-8. *Laying out a joint freehand.*

Illus. 6-9. *If the board is 1 inch thick or thicker, make parallel rows of biscuits. Shown here are the slots for the biscuits.*

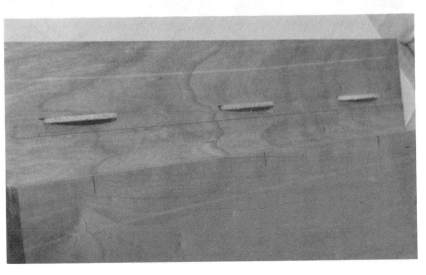

Illus. 6-10. *Making the marks to one side of the member. The pencil lines show the edge of the joint.*

Cutting the Slot

Always clamp the board to be cut or slotted. The cutting operation is accomplished by pressing the vertical fence against the board to be cut (Illus. 6-11 and 6-12). Sharp tips on the fence hold the machine in place. With one hand on the handle and the other on the body turn on the motor and push the body forward at a steady pace. The motor assembly and the cutter are spring-loaded; with the forward movement, the cutter will slide out to cut a groove in the wood. The chips are ejected through an exhaust port on the right hand of the machine base into either a dust bag or dust-collector hose.

Depth-of-cut adjustment biscuit joiners have three or more standard cutting depths to accommodate the three standard (#0, 10, and 20) biscuit sizes. Once you have made the proper adjustment for one biscuit size on your machine, the other two are automatically set correctly. On most machines, the depth-adjustment housing is located on the right side of the machine. The three biscuit sizes are marked and calibrated on the housing. A spring-loaded shaft allows you to select the proper size.

With the tool unplugged, check your depth of cut. If you are using the joiner for the first time, it

Illus. 6-11. *When cutting a board, press the vertical fence of the joiner against the board.*

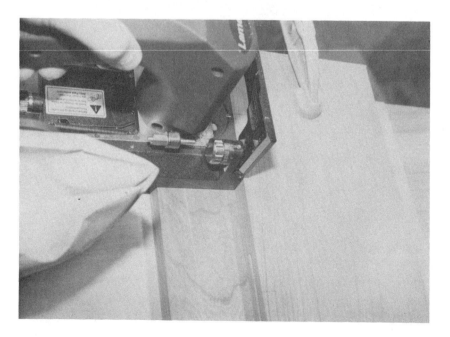

Illus. 6-12. *A close-up of a horizontal cut.*

has been set at the factory, and the depth of cut should be okay. After you have checked and adjusted the depth of cut the first time, you are set for cutting all three sizes of biscuits, and you need only occasionally check the setting.

To check the depth of cut, clamp a piece of scrap wood securely to a firm surface. Make a test cut and insert a #10 biscuit. The slot should be deep enough to allow slightly more than half of the #10 biscuit into the slot. This additional fraction of depth will allow for proper vertical alignment of the wood being joined. If the depth setting needs adjustment, move the knurled nuts forward for a shallower cut or rearwards for a deeper cut. To make an adjustment, you'll probably need a six-millimetre wrench that is not supplied with the joiner to adjust the depth-stop nuts in or out, as shown in Illus. 6-13.

It is also easy to check the depth of cut with a #20 biscuit rather than with a ruler. A #20 biscuit

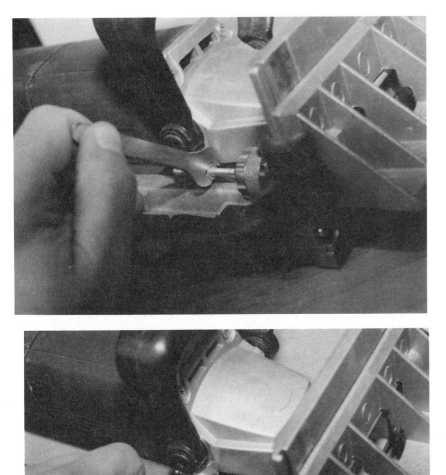

Illus. 6-13 and 6-14. To make the depth-of-cut adjustment, you sometimes have to use a six-millimetre wrench to adjust the depth-stop nuts.

Illus. 6-14.

is ⅞ inch wide, so a slot that is slightly less than ½ inch wide makes a good fit. The number of grooves cut into each joint depends on the thickness of the wood. Generally one biscuit is sufficient for ¾-inch stock. It is often a good idea to use two biscuits for 2-inch stock and more for thicker boards. The size or length of the biscuit used is determined by the width of the joint. Use the largest biscuits possible. When making edge-mitre cuts in ¾-inch stock or frame-mitre cuts in narrow stock, use the smaller biscuits. When gluing tabletops or cutting boards or similar edge-to-edge projects, the more biscuits you use, the stronger the joint will be.

Chapter 7

MAKING EDGE-TO-EDGE JOINTS

Edge-to-edge joints are made by mating the edges of boards. How important is it that you biscuit-join edge-to-edge joints? If your stock is perfectly flat and you have been careful enough while gluing that you can ensure that the joined sections stay flat, it is not important that you biscuit-join edge-to-edge joints. Often, however, stock is not perfectly flat, so alignment of the boards can be a problem. Also, we're often in too much of a hurry to glue only two pieces at a time, which often happens when assembling panels, for example. Thus, in these two instances biscuit-joining can be of considerable value.

The edge-to-edge joint (Illus. 7-1) is one of the most basic and easiest joints to construct. The biscuits in an edge-to-edge joint are essentially splines that add tremendous strength to the joint. When you are gluing up panels using biscuit joints, you'll spend only an extra half minute per joint cutting slots and inserting the biscuits. The results are joints that hold tightly without sliding around, and that will be flat and true even before you plane or sand them.

To ensure the flattest possible work, glue only two pairs of pieces together at a time. Using this method, follow these easy steps for efficient edge-

Illus. 7-1.   *Edge-to-edge joints are among the easiest joints to make. Shown here is an edge-joined board. Note the layout for the biscuits. I made the marks more prominent than usual so they appear in the photograph.*

to-edge gluing when making panels: Start with opposite sides of a wide panel and glue two pairs of pieces together at a time until you have one pair left, and then glue those pieces together.

Lay out the wood pieces as they are to be assembled. With a pencil, mark the locations on the mating pieces of wood for the cuts. Mark the boards to be joined about 2½ inches from either end and about 8–10 inches apart between them (Illus. 7-2). This joint will be stronger if you use multiple biscuits placed close together (Illus. 7-3).

After laying out the marks, cut the slots. Cutting the slots for edge-joined biscuits is most easily done by placing the fixed-angle cutting guide or the flap fence at 90 degrees over the edge as shown in Illus. 7-4 and cutting the edge and ends.

Adjust the fence so that the slot for the biscuit is centered.

For 2-inch-thick stock you may wish to stack biscuits (Illus. 7-5). In this case, simply readjust the fence for the second cut above or below the first. Leave a small space between each cut. Place the fence against the surface of the wood. Align the red indicator mark on the fence with the pencil marks on the wood. With a steady motion, push the machine body forward and make the cut. Repeat this process for each marked area on the wood pieces.

Place biscuits in the slots of one board (Illus. 7-6). Bring both mating pieces together. Make certain there is enough vertical play in the boards to allow for proper alignment. Disassemble the

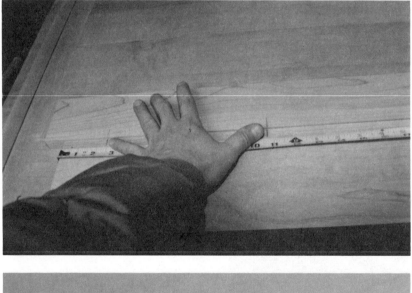

Illus. 7-2. *Mark out the biscuit locations about 2½ inches from either end and about 8–10 inches apart between them. Your spread hands can be a good gauge of this distance.*

Illus. 7-3. *An edge-to-edge joint will be stronger if you use multiple biscuits.*

Illus. 7-4. *Cutting the slots for edge-joining in a narrow board. Boards this narrow don't really have to be biscuited together unless you have to use the wider pieces immediately.*

Illus. 7-5. *If working with 2-inch-thick boards, you may wish to stack biscuits. This joint has stacked biscuits.*

Illus. 7-6. *A close-up of a biscuit placed in the slot on one board.*

boards, glue the slots (Illus. 7-7), and reassemble and clamp the boards. To ensure the flattest possible work, glue only two pieces together at a time (Illus. 7-8).

When edge-gluing panels, insert the biscuits about ten inches apart. This interval is an estimate that is based on practical experience (Illus. 7-9–7-11). In my shop, I tried three different placement options when gluing panels for a commercial project. On one pair of boards I placed a biscuit approximately every 8 inches. Many biscuits were used and this seemed to be a waste of material. On the next pair of boards, I placed biscuits approximately every 12 inches. Those biscuits were spaced far enough apart that the joined materials "wandered" a bit and were slightly un-

even. Biscuits clamped at 10-inch intervals proved to be just about right. If you're working with stock that's exceptionally flat, your placement may be even farther apart than the 10 inches suggested here, but if the materials don't match for any reason (for example, if you're trying to include one slightly warped or bowed panel into an otherwise flat top) you might reduce the interval to as little as five or six inches.

Biscuit joining like that used for edge-to-edge joining not only ensures flatter panels, but it also allows you to remove clamps much sooner than you otherwise might be able to. Since it becomes much harder to run out of clamps, your workshop will function more smoothly.

Illus. 7-7.   Remove the glue from edge joints while it is still the consistency of cottage cheese.

Illus. 7-8.   Even when using biscuit joints, glue up your panels one at a time. The six panels you see here will become a single tabletop.

Illus. 7-9. The biscuit on the right is properly positioned, but the one on the left is much too close to the edge.

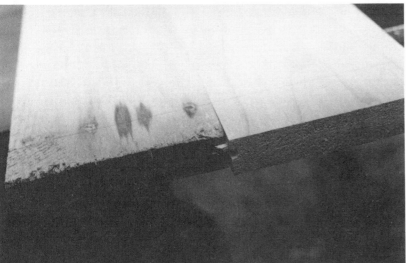

Illus. 7-10. An end view of the joint shown in Illus. 7-9.

Illus. 7-11. A cut-off biscuit joint is very unattractive, so plan your panels so you can avoid sawing through the joint.

Chapter 8

MAKING BUTT JOINTS

A butt joint is a joint in which the edge or end of one board is butted against another board (Illus. 8-1). Butt joints are the weakest joints in woodworking. Normally, when you make a butt joint you are mating the end grain of one board with the face or edge grain of another board, so the glue surface is poor. However, with a joiner and the use of biscuits you can create a tenon effect between the mating pieces of wood which creates a very strong joint.

Corner Butt Joints

Making corner butt joints is much quicker than making dowels or dovetails. There are two ways to make the corner butt joints used on internal members such as partitions, dividers, etc. Both these methods will be described here. Decide upon

which you'll use regularly only after you have tried them. Each method has its advantages.

In both methods, accurate setup is the key to accurate work. Align the two pieces of wood to form the horizontal or flat board and the vertical board (Illus. 8-2). The vertical board has the end grain. Draw a centerline on the two boards where you want the biscuit slots centered. The joint is laid out exactly the same for both methods. Mark lines 2½ inches from the end of the joint and 4–6 inches apart between them. Make parallel rows (one or more from each side) of biscuits if the workpieces are one inch thick or thicker.

Next, cut the joints. In both methods make all of the cuts in the vertical board first, and then the horizontal board. In the first method, cut a slot on the face of one of the pair of pieces to be joined, and then cut a slot on the edge of the other piece (Illus. 8-3). This method puts the slots exactly

Illus. 8-1.   A marked-out butt joint.

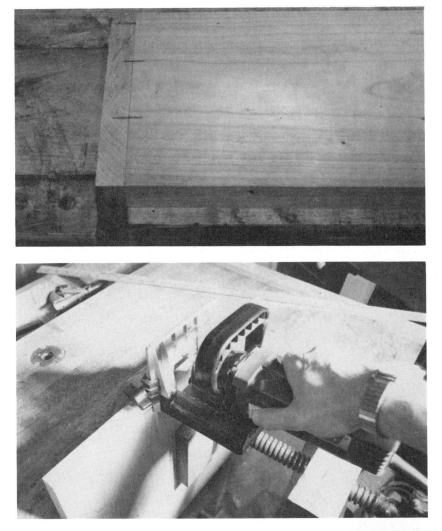

Illus. 8-2.   Align the two pieces of wood to form the horizontal or flat board and the vertical board.

Illus. 8-3.   Cutting an edge on one of the mating pieces.

where they are needed, but if you're working more quickly than carefully, the joint pieces can be misaligned if you don't cut accurately into the face of the material.

In the second method, lay out a piece of material adjacent to your work that is the same thickness as the material being joined. This shim material supports the machine as it works through the

Illus. 8-4 (right).   In the second method, you first stand the two pieces to be joined edge to edge, perpendicular to one another. Then tip the vertical edge piece over on its axis. It helps to scribe a line at the inside edge to ensure accurate positioning. Then clamp the vertical piece to the horizontal piece so the surfaces to be joined are at right angles to one another.

Illus. 8-5.   *The layout for the corner butt joint and the shim piece (bottom) that will keep all the cuts square.*

Illus. 8-6.   *A front view of the vertical slots with the shim in place. This method of cutting butt joints is slightly more time-consuming to set up than the first method described and illustrated in Illus. 8-3.*

Illus. 8-7.   *A close-up rear view of cutting vertical slots with the shim in place.*

joinery. Stand the pieces edge to edge, perpendicular to one another. Carefully lay the vertical edge piece over on its axis, which is the inside edge of the joint (Illus. 8-4). Scribe a line at the inside edge to ensure accurate positioning. Clamp the vertical piece to the horizontal piece so the surfaces to be joined are at right angles to one another. Mark out the joints again two inches from either end and about four inches apart in between. Mark out the joints only at the very edge of the horizontal piece as shown in Illus. 8-5.

Using the extra piece to support the joiner squarely, first cut the vertical slots (Illus. 8-6 and 8-7). Then, after sweeping away those chips, cut the horizontal slots (Illus. 8-8 and 8-9). The finished joint is shown in Illus. 8-10 and 8-11.

Whichever method you choose to cut the joints, they glue up alike. Before gluing them up, however, test-fit the entire assembly with dry biscuits. If the pieces all fit, proceed with gluing the slots and adding the biscuits. After unclamping the pieces, put glue into the slots, insert the biscuits, and assemble them. There is no need to glue the end grain to the long grain, so it will be very worthwhile if you do some preliminary finishing work *before* assembly. Glue the pieces as follows: Lay one of the pieces that will have a biscuit on its side. Glue only the slots. Either run

Illus. 8-8 and 8-9. Cutting horizontal slots with the shim piece in place.

Illus. 8-9.

Illus. 8-10 and 8-11.   The finished butt joint.

Illus. 8-11.

a fair bead of glue down each side of the slot or use a glue bottle made for biscuit joining. Next, insert the biscuits into each slot. Then glue the slots on the pieces to be attached, and attach them immediately. Apply the glue and biscuits to the next pieces. Continue adding glue and biscuits to the slots. Proceed in this fashion for the entire project. Make sure that the assembly is possible according to the way you are proceeding.

Offset Butt Joints

When joining table legs and rails, it may be necessary to offset the rails to the center of the legs (Illus. 8-12). In this case, the fence needs to be readjusted to slot the legs properly. If you wish a ⅛-inch offset, readjust the joiner's auxiliary fence up ⅛ inch after all the rails have been cut to make the appropriate cut in the legs. For example, align the rail flush with the outside of the leg to make your mark on both pieces of wood for the center of the biscuit cut (Illus. 8-13). Make the cut in the ends of the rails. Adjust the fence up ⅛ inch and keep the horizontal fence on the outside edge of the leg; make the appropriate slots in the legs. If you want a ⅜-inch offset, move the fence ⅜ inch away from the blade. Other sizes of offset require corresponding adjustments.

Offset joints are cut in the same manner as regular butted joints. Lay them out together, and then cut them with a shim in the joiner at one of the matching cuts. For example, the apron and legs on a table aren't usually flush with each other. You can set the apron back from the legs by setting

Illus. 8-12.   When joining table legs and rails, it may be necessary to offset the rails to the center of the legs.

Illus. 8-13.   To mark both pieces of wood for the center of the biscuit cut, align the rail flush with the outside of the leg.

a piece of ⅛-inch-thick Masonite (or another material of another thickness) between the apron and the height-adjustment fence on the joiner's faceplate.

T-Joints

T-joints are standard butt joints used for internal pieces (Illus. 8-14). They are the ideal joint for installing fixed-position shelves and dividers. They are used when it is necessary to add support members to strengthen a frame. They are called T-joints because when you look at them from their ends, they are shaped like the letter T.

Making T-joints to join internal carcass members is only marginally different from making corner butt joints. The difference is that when you lay out an interior joint, as on a drawer frame, shelf, etc., lay out the joint to one side of the member rather than to its center (Illus. 8-15). You lay out the joint from one side because that side will be the axis of the "hinge" on which you lay the board down, flush to the other, so that you can cut the matching slots in or near the middle of the joints. In other words, if you want to center a ¾-inch-thick piece exactly, lay it out ⅜ inch to the side from which you plan to do work. This will produce a centered joint.

The pieces must be laid out logically. Since you will be marking the sides of the joints (at their top or bottom, and front or back), use the same side all the time, as shown in Illus. 8-14. Be sure to label where the pieces go. If you forget the assembly order, that will lead to trouble, especially if you aren't cutting your slots exactly in the middle of

Illus. 8-14.   *A T-joint. T-joints are lined up at their top or bottom edges. Use the same edge on every joint in an assembly. Notice the joint registration line.*

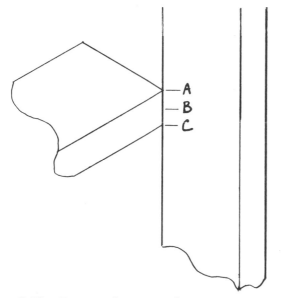

Illus. 8-15.   *Lay out the interior butt joints at A or C, not at B.*

the work. As in the preferred method for the corner butt joint, first cut the vertical slots and then the horizontal slots. Then glue the slots, insert the biscuits, and assemble the joints.

Let's use the example of putting a shelf in a bookcase to illustrate the role of the T-joint. The shelf represents the horizontal board, and the bookcase side is the vertical board. We must put slots in the end of the horizontal shelf board. That's the same application as used in edge-to-edge joining. Putting slots in the side of the verti-

cal board, however, requires using the joiner to make T-joints.

Lay the vertical board down and place the horizontal board where you want it to fit. Draw light pencil marks along the edges of where the boards meet. Draw marks on both boards, indicating the center of the slot locations (Illus. 8-16). Adjust the fence to center the cut in the horizontal board and make all the cuts (Illus. 8-17). Remove the horizontal fence. Notice the red centering mark on the vertical fence. Set the machine aside. Use compressed air to remove the chips caused by making the horizontal cuts (Illus. 8-18).

Centering the cuts on the vertical board requires practice and accuracy. It is necessary to clamp a fence or support board to the vertical board in order to make the cuts accurately. Determine where you want the center cuts to be made. If you are going to center the cuts in the horizontal board, and you want the same fit in the vertical board, measure the distance from the bottom of the cut in the horizontal board. Clamp the wooden fence on the vertical board the same distance from where you want the cut. Rest the joiner on the fence, and align the red centering mark on the joiner with the centering mark on the wood. Make the plunge cut (Illus. 8-19 and 8-20).

The bottom lip of the blade is located $5/16$ inch from the bottom of the machine. If you are working with a three-inch-thick board, and you need two biscuits one inch apart, simply use a one-inch

Illus. 8-16.   Draw light pencil marks on both boards, indicating the center of the slot locations.

Illus. 8-17.   Making a horizontal cut in the board.

Illus. 8-18.   Use compressed air to remove the chips that resulted from the horizontal cuts. This will ensure that the joiner will rest flatly and squarely on the work.

Illus. 8-19 and 8-20 (left and above).   Making the vertical cut.

spacer board between the machine and the wooden fence for the second cut. Any other variation must take into account the distance from the bottom of the machine to the bottom of the blade. It's that simple.

Next, apply the glue, insert the biscuits, and assemble the pieces (Illus. 8-21 and 8-22). All the pieces that go between the horizontal and vertical piece must be added at once, and you must assemble the joint from the inside out. Failing to assemble all members that were cut from the same part of the logical sequence will mean that you will have to omit those parts because they can't be added in between biscuit-joined work.

There is no way to overemphasize the importance of partial finishing before beginning biscuit joinery, particularly when joining those internal members. At the very least, sand with all but 180,

Illus. 8-21.   After making the cuts, apply the glue and insert the biscuits.

Illus. 8-22.   The assembled joint. Woodworkers should sand the registration marks off before gluing, to make finishing easier.

220, and any higher-number grit of sandpaper. Assembly has to be done so quickly that failure to do the prefinishing will make some of the finishing painstakingly difficult to do. After the sanding is done, assemble the pieces without doing any joining. The fit must be almost—if not exactly—perfect. If it's not, correct any imperfections in the fit at this point.

These precautions also apply when you are making a large project. The most difficult thing about making carcass units in the small shop is cutting the material accurately to both squareness and to dimensions needed. If you're working with expensive panel stock, it may be worthwhile to have your lumberyard do as much of the cutting as they can be expected to do—if they can do such a cutting accurately.

Chapter 9

MAKING MITRE JOINTS

A mitre joint is made by cutting two pieces at an angle and fitting them together (Illus. 9-1). There are different types of mitre joints. The joiner can be used to make flat and edge mitres. Flat mitres are used in picture frames (Illus. 9-2). Edge mitres are used when you are making boxes or items where you don't want the end grain of wood to show (Illus. 9-3). Biscuit joinery makes mitre joints especially strong. In fact, a mitre joint with biscuits is much stronger and more handsome than one that has just been glued or glued and nailed.

Making the mitre joint consists of cutting the mitres on the stock, cutting the slots for the biscuit joint, gluing the slots, inserting the biscuits, and assembling the pieces.

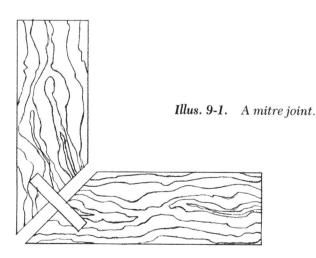

Illus. 9-1. A mitre joint.

Cutting Mitres on Stock

The most difficult thing about mitre joints is making the mitre cuts on the stock. Table saws are generally used to make mitre cuts. The standard mitre gauge on a table saw isn't much good for crosscutting wide stock. An alternative is to clamp a straightedge accurately to the carcass piece and use the edge of the saw as a fence. This works well, but it provides ample possibilities for imprecision, and it is important that the pieces correspond to one another if the joints are to work.

Following are the steps for cutting mitres on stock using a straightedge:

1. Measure and mark the length you wish to cut. If your setup is less than square and true, the results will be imperfect, but probably still better than when using the crosscutting fence alone.

2. Check the measurement from the edge of the saw table to the blade. On most American saws, this is exactly 18 inches.

3. Mark 18¾ inches down from your cutting line if you are cutting ¾-inch-thick material. If not, add whatever is the thickness of the stock to the 18 inches. Then clamp a straight board across

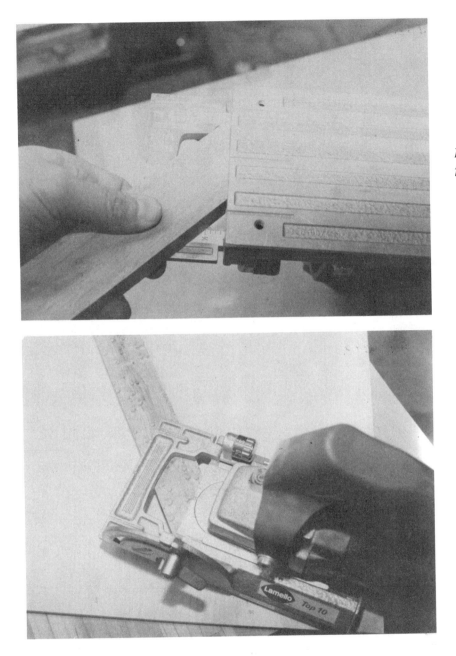

Illus. 9-2. *Flat mitres are used in picture frames.*

Illus. 9-3. *Edge mitres are used on projects in which you don't want the wood's end grain to show.*

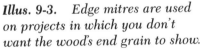

the marks. Check and double-check that the board is square. For this use, I prefer a 2 × 2-inch board that is perfectly straight.

4. Remove the rip fence from the table saw and make the cut using the edge of the saw table as a guide. This is much more accurate than using most mitre gauges for this kind of cut. You can square imperfect cuts by loosening one of the clamps and moving the board ever so slightly.

A table saw with a sliding table (Illus. 9-4) will cut mitres even more accurately than the clamping device described above. While such tables have long been available for European table saws, they only recently have become available for some Delta saws and for some of the better Asian imports.

Illus. 9-4. *A table saw with a sliding table cuts mitres very accurately.*

Making Slot Cuts

As mentioned earlier, a flat mitre is used on picture frames (Illus. 9-5 and 9-6). Such a mitre needs a blind biscuit, that is, a biscuit that no one will be able to see after the project has been completed. The information in this section specifically concerns cutting flat mitres for use in picture frames, but it can be applied to making any flat mitre.

Making a picture frame can be simplified with the biscuit joiner as long as each mitred piece is at least 1¾ inches wide so the diagonal portions of the mitres are 2½ inches apart. This way, slot cuts can be made in the mitres for the biscuits without cutting through their sides. I have found it best to cut the biscuit slots before cutting the rabbets which hold the picture and the glass.

After the mitres are cut and the pieces are ready for joining, mark the stock on the mitred faces, adjust your joiner's depth of cut, and cut your slots, two inches from the edges and about 4 inches on center between them. Position the joiner carefully on the narrow work (Illus. 9-7–9-9). Cut slowly, to ensure precision. The slots should more or less extend throughout these mitres. Line up the center bar of the joiner with the pencil marks. Make certain the wood is clamped down and the 45-degree fence is flat on the horizontal wood surface. Make all your cuts,

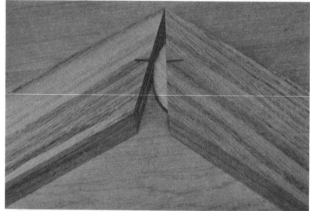

Illus. 9-5. *A picture-frame mitre before it is closed.*

Illus. 9-6. *A closed picture-frame mitre.*

Illus. 9-7. *When cutting picture-frame mitres or for other very narrow joining projects, use a biscuit joiner that has a non-skid surface on its faceplate. This ensures that the joiner will not skip when you are cutting the slots.*

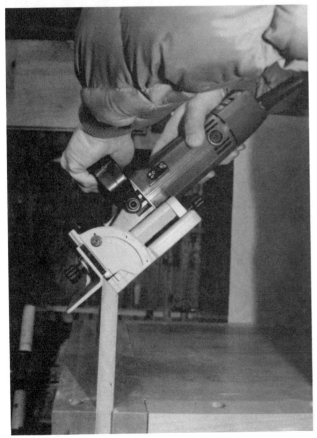

Illus. 9-8. *Making a mitre cut. A two-handed approach is the best one to take when cutting any joints, but especially when cutting mitre joints. It's important that the joints line up square and tight.*

Illus. 9-9. *A close-up look at cutting a frame mitre.*

insert the biscuits, and dry-assemble them. If the pieces fit, add glue in the slots and clamp the biscuits in place. Web clamps are great for box assemblies.

Forty-five-degree mitre cuts are best cut with a joiner with a flap face so the joints register from the outside of the joiner (Illus. 9-10–9-12). Use the center bar of the fence to center the cut. Make the cuts close to the inside of the mitre because these will be stronger joints. Care must be excercised not to cut too deep. When cutting 1-inch-thick stock, use the setting for the smallest biscuits.

Illus. 9-10. *The best way to make 45-degree mitre cuts is with a joiner with a flap face.*

Illus. 9-12. *Note the registration marks on the joiner aligned with the marked-out joint.*

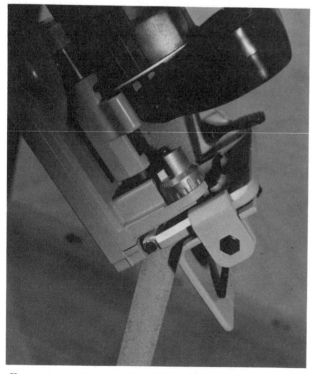

Illus. 9-11. *The notch in this biscuit joiner makes cutting at 45-degree angles very easy.*

Using Joiners Without Flap Faces

You can cut any angle of mitre with a joiner that does not have a flap face by adding a compensating wedge (Illus. 9-13 and 9-14). This wedge should be cut so as to have the same angle of the mitres of the wood to be joined. For example, to join two pieces of wood each with a 15-degree mitre, you'll need a wedge with a 15-degree right angle. You can attach the wedge to the bottom of the fence with the use of a double-sided tape or hot-melt adhesive. For large production jobs, drill holes in the fence and attach the wedge with screws. Using a joiner *with* a flap face like the Freud JS-102 permits making a variety of angle joints without using a wedge.

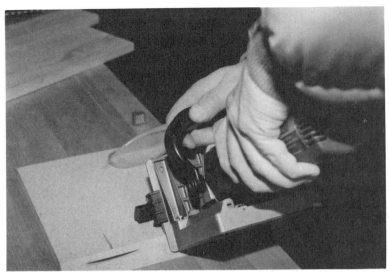

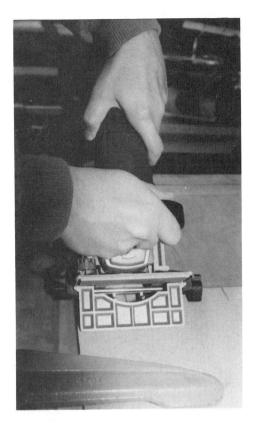

Illus. 9-13 (above). Cutting at 45-degree angles with a fixed-faceplate joiner is awkward. If using such a joiner, add a wedge cut at the same angle as the mitres to the bottom of the fence with double-sided tape or hot-melt adhesive. Illus. 9-14 (right). Another view showing cutting at a 45-degree angle with a fixed-faceplate joiner.

Cutting Mitres on the Outside of the Joint

The Porter-Cable 555 joiner was the first joiner which permitted joining mitres of unequal thickness by locating the slots from the outsides rather than the insides of the pieces. This way, the outsides of the mitres meet, which is most likely more important than having the insides of the joint meet. The popularity of these outside-joined mitres caused the manufacturers of other joiners to start selling joiners in which mitres could be joined from the outside. Today, virtually every joiner with a flap fence can be made to join mitres from the inside or outside of the joint.

There are two advantages to having mitres that fit at the outside. First, if you have mitres that fit at the inside and you have to cut the outside flush, there will be some end-grain visible, and this will reveal that your joinery is less than precise. Second, when cutting inside mitres, unless the operator works very carefully, there's a great chance he will cut the joint out of square, thus destroying the fit of the joint.

Illus. 9-15. The Porter-Cable 555 joiner was the first joiner to cut 45-degree mitres from the outside of the joint.

Illus. 9-16. This view shows the joiner indexing against the outside of the joint.

Chapter 10

SPECIALIZED JOINT-MAKING INFORMATION

The information in this chapter will help you in specific instances when cutting joints.

Laying Out Narrow Work

The newest joiners on the market are better at cutting narrow work than the older models. The older machines have a pair of spring-loaded pins and have to contact the work with both pins to remain stable. These pins were superseded by rubber bumpers, which in turn gave way to non-slip surfaces. The newest joiners have nonslip surfaces, which make cutting narrow work very easy. If you have a good eye, you can lay out narrow pieces sometimes without even marking the work; the guide marks on the machine will show the outer limits of the workpiece and permit you to center the piece quickly using only your eyes as a guide (Illus. 10-1).

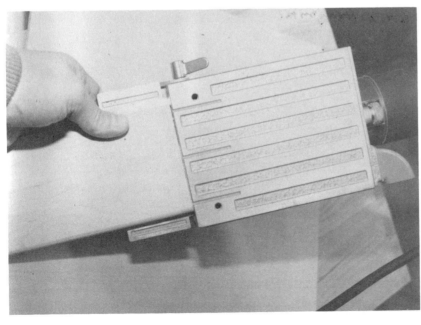

Illus. 10-1. *Using the guide marks on the joiner, you can center it on the workpiece using only your eyes as a guide.*

Cutting Joints at Nonstandard Angles

Joints other than 45- or 90-degree joints can be cut almost as easily as 45- or 90-degree joints. Cutting these joints is simply a matter of making an appropriate shim and fastening it to the fence of your joiner. Hot glue and duct tape work well for this fastening (Illus. 10-2), but you may want to screw these shims in place if you have many such joints to cut.

The shims should be about the same size as the face of your fixed-angle faceplate, generally about 2 × 5 inches, and can be attached to either the square side of the fence or the mitre face of the board, whichever you find easier and more accurate. After you have removed the glued and taped shims, you'll find that cleanup is surprisingly easy.

Illus. 10-3 shows the making of a nonstandard angle joint. A 15-degree shim is taped to the square side of the fence to make a 30-degree joint. While you could also tape it to the mitre face, doing it this way would create a joint that does not have a gap. You can adjust the taped-on gauge for this application simply by setting the front of it on the workbench and then screwing it in place. This is a simple joint, but it can be used in many applications.

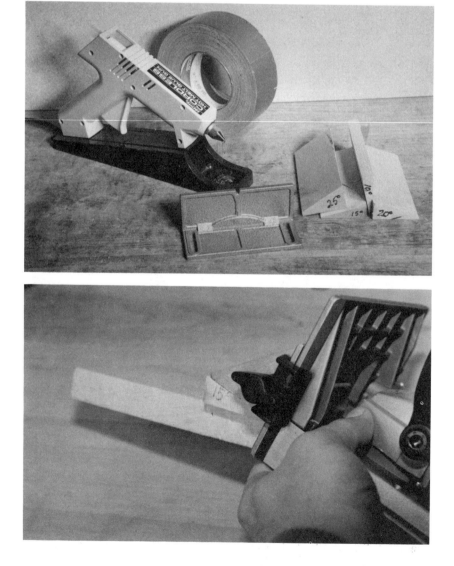

Illus. 10-2.   Shown here is all the equipment needed to mount the various angle blocks. Clockwise from the top are the following: duct tape, the shop-made angle blocks, the fixed-angle faceplate, and a glue gun.

Illus. 10-3.   Here a 15-degree shim is taped to the square side of the joiner's fence to make a 30-degree joint.

Making Face-Frame Joints

Kitchen cabinetmakers, among other sheet-stock users, will find the joiner useful for making face-frame joints. These are the joints that attach the hardwood face frame to the carcass, which is usually made of plywood (Illus. 10-4). To set up for a face-frame joint, make jig blocks as wide as the offset shoulders, as shown in Illus. 10-5. This block is the basic setup for the entire operation.

Make the cuts in the frame piece with the joiner resting on the base against the jig block, as shown in Illus. 10-6. Then cut the face piece with the fence resting on the edge as shown in Illus. 10-7. Illus. 10-8 demonstrates the perfect centering that this technique delivers.

Illus. 10-4 (right). A face frame. Face-frame joints attach the hardwood face frame to the usually plywood carcass.

Illus. 10-5. Laying out a simple face-frame joint. Note the jig block on the far right.

Illus. 10-6. Make the cuts in the frame piece with the joiner resting on the base against the jig block.

Illus. 10-7. The next cut is made with the fence resting on the edge of the face frame.

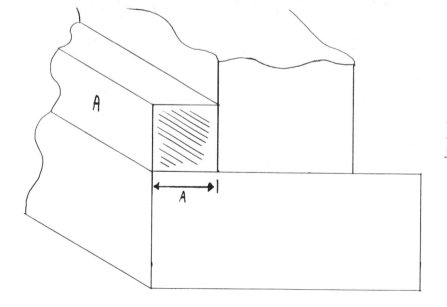

Illus. 10-8. Shim A is "A" inches square by at least the length of the joiner's faceplate.

Gauge Blocks

A set of gauge blocks for wood of the most common thicknesses will save you a great deal of time when using a joiner (Illus. 10-9). First, these gauges are better to use than the joiner's square slides because the slots on the mating pieces must be exactly parallel and the gauges can ensure that they are. Second, this set of blocks will also make it easier to set up the joiner for stacking biscuits

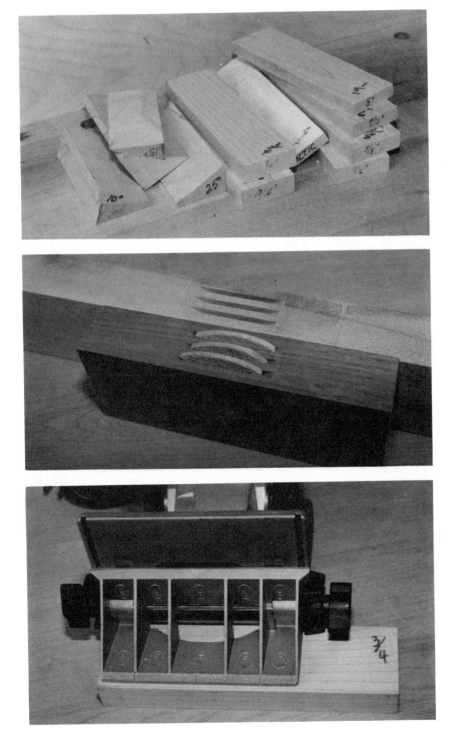

Illus. 10-9.   A stack of carefully made gauge blocks will be a valuable time saver.

Illus. 10-10.   When glued up, this stacked joint will be incredibly strong.

Illus. 10-11.   Here the faceplate is set on the gauge block with the base of the joiner flat on the bench.

when you need mechanical strength in the joint, particularly when joining thicker stock (Illus. 10-10). Third, the blocks can be combined for thicker pieces, or you can choose various-sized blocks when you want to stagger biscuits in joints that will be heavily stressed.

To use the gauge blocks, loosen the adjustable faceplate and set it on the gauge block with the base of the joiner flat on the bench (Illus. 10-11).

The blocks should be 2 × 7 inches, so that they can be big enough to fully support the fixed-angle faceplate and still leave its label exposed; the label shows the measurement of the block. My set of blocks runs by eighths of an inch from 1/8 to 7/8 inch thick, with a block of Baltic birch plywood included for good measure. My lumber dealer supplies this stock as 1/2 inch thick, but it is not.

Chapter II

PROJECTS

You can use the information provided in the previous chapters to build the assortment of projects provided here. Parts and tools lists, assembly drawings, and cutting instructions are provided for each project, which range in complexity from a simple planter to a chest. The more simple projects are presented first.

Planter

Here is a simple yet practical project that just begs for you to modify it to suit more practical dimensions for yourself (Illus. 11-1–11-3). Few projects will do more to dress up the outside of your home for anywhere near this project's low cost.

Materials Used

I used two 6-foot-long pieces of 1-inch-thick × 8-inch-wide cedar to cut a 32-inch-long planter (Illus. 11-4). Choose your stock carefully. Some of the cedar I rejected had 10-inch-long splits at the ends (Illus. 11-5). The cedar came from the lumberyard with one planed face and one rough side (Illus. 11-6). I built the planter with the rough side out. The planter, after all, will be an outside project, and when it is shown with its rough side out, looks more suitable for outdoor use. Also, using the planed side on the outside of the planter would mean some extra time sanding out the planer marks.

Illus. 11-1. *You can modify the dimensions for this planter to build one that meets your specific needs.*

Illus. 11-2.   *This planter is inexpensive to make and is attractive.*

Top View

17/8"

73/8"

8"

32"

Side View

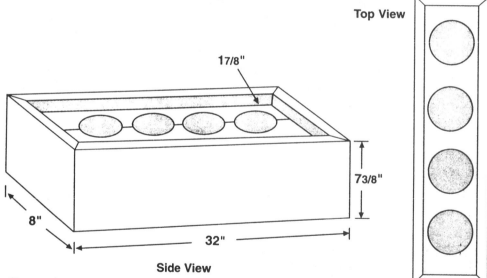

Illus. 11-3.   *Drawing of planter.*

Parts List for Planter

Part	Length	Width	Thickness	Quantity
Front and Back	32"	7⅜"	⅞"	2
Sides	8"	7⅜"	⅞"	2
Insert (All edges are trimmed to a thickness of ½ to ¾".)	30¹⁵⁄₁₆"	7⅜"	⅞"	1

Tools and Materials for Planter
Table saw, hand-held circular saw, or sabre saw to make the crosscuts,
    mitre cuts, and rip cuts
Router with ¾-inch straight bit or dado set for table saw
Biscuit joiner with eight #20 biscuits
Layout tools
Clamps
Glue
Finishing products

Illus. 11-4. Measure the flower pots you plan to use to get an overall size of the project.

Illus. 11-5. Buy enough stock so that you can cut around knots like this. If your mitre joint were cut right over the knot, it might not hold up.

Illus. 11-6. This Western red cedar has a rough (bottom) and a planed side. The planer marks are visible.

Construction Procedures

Cut your pieces to length, and then mitre each piece to be joined at each corner. Assuming that you have cut the pieces to length square, set the cut narrower, to the thickness of the board. I moved the cut ⅞ inch closer to the blade to cut my ⅞-inch-thick stock perfectly. Keep the mitre gauge on your table saw set perfectly square.

Cut with a biscuit joiner to fit two #20 biscuits at each corner (Illus. 11-7 and 11-8). Then cut the dado for the insert all the way around the four pieces (Illus. 11-9–11-11). Part of the rationale for mitring the pieces is that mitred corners greatly simplify inserting the planter board later on. To prevent having an odd-sized dado, cut a standard-sized dado and then trim the edges of the insert material to fit it. Cut the dado 1⅞ inches from the top.

The insert is as long as the dado inside the mitres on the long piece, and as wide as the dadoes on the inside of the end pieces. Cut 1/16 to 1/32 inch less than those sizes, and then trim the ends to fit the dado.

Rip the insert in half, lengthwise, and then set the two pieces together so you can use this fresh cut as the centerline. Lay out circles for flower pots (Illus. 11-12). Cut them with a hand-held or stationary sabre saw or a scroll saw. Cutting these

circles imperfectly with a saw is far faster and safer than cutting them with a fly cutter, and most of us don't have very large hole-cutting saws or bits. As Illus. 11-13 indicates, these circles don't have to be perfectly round to hold the pots. I cut the holes to hold pots ranging from 4¾ to 6 inches in diameter.

If you wish, cut a scallop at the bottom edge of the front face of the project before you begin to assemble it (Illus. 11-14). Lay it out by eye, but carefully with a ruler and a good curve of the size you're trying to reproduce. This scallop can be cut with a scroll saw, a hand-operated sabre saw, or even a muscle-powered coping saw. Some woodworkers will omit this step without harming the project's appearance. Since the project is being built with nominal 1 × 8-inch stock, which is in fact only 7⅜ inches wide, the scallop probably shouldn't be much over 1½ inches wide.

After all the pieces have been cut out, put glue in the biscuit slots (Illus. 11-15), and set the biscuits in place, assembling the entire unit in the process. The pair of inserts should "float" nicely in the channel created by the dado (Illus. 11-16). A bit of clamping may be required to hold the unit together until the glue sets. While we're using only white carpenter's glue, and only in the biscuit holes, we're confident that the joints will hold for many years, especially if we put a couple of good

Illus. 11-7 (above left). Cutting the slots in the mitred ends. *Illus. 11-8 (above right).* The cut slots in the mitred ends.

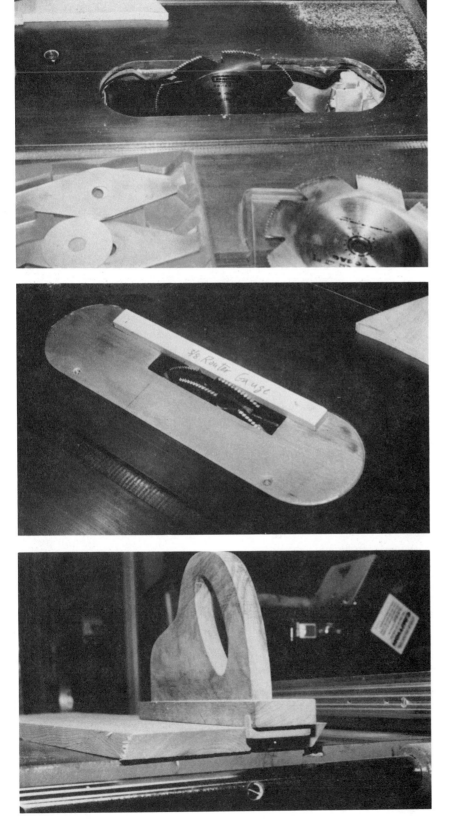

Illus. 11-9.   *Set up the dado head to cut the channel for the flower pot holes.*

Illus. 11-10.   *Set the depth of the dado cut with a preset measuring gauge.*

Illus. 11-11.   *Be sure to use push blocks and all other available safety equipment when you cut the dadoes on the table saw.*

Illus. 11-12 (left). With a large compass, mark the holes you will cut for the flower pots. The insert has been ripped, and the stationary end of the compass is resting in the kerf. *Illus. 11-13 (above right).* The insert in place in the planter, showing how the pots will fit.

Illus. 11-14 (left). If you plan to have scallops or other design elements along the bottom edge of the planter, a scroll saw is the ideal tool to cut them with because it will give you the neatest work that is most ready to finish. A hand-held sabre saw or a muscle-powered coping saw would work, but both would leave rougher edges than the scroll saw. Be sure to cut these design elements before mitring and assembling the project.

Illus. 11-15. *This is really all the glue you need to hold these biscuit joints.*

Illus. 11-16. *The insert in place in the planter, showing how the pots will fit.*

Illus. 11-17. *The finished planter.*

coats of some water-resistant finish on both the inside and out!

This project illustrates one of the main advantages of making a dry-fitting of biscuit joints. It allows you to reassemble the project to make it more attractive. With this project, you can determine while dry-fitting the biscuits whether you want to have the planter facing up one way and having the pots show or want the planter to face 180 degrees opposite the first position, with the pots completely inside the planter. I prefer the look of the project with the pots sitting lower in the box, so that little of the "workings" of the project are visible to the casual observer.

This planter presents several advantages over the older style of planter. For starters, it is much lighter. The flowers are easier to replace because there is no digging in mass flower beds. This planter is no more difficult to make than the standard dirt-filled planter, and requires far less maintenance because there won't be a constant wetness in contact with the entire inner surface. Thus, it is more likely to hold its finish.

Knockdown Bookcase

With the vast number of Americans on the move every year, it's important to have some furniture that is easy to move as well as handsome. Here's a cherry bookcase that can be built and finished in a weekend, and which has the added virtue of being collapsible for easy shipping (Illus. 11-18 and 11-19). The working parts of the case are the pair of small open "boxes" which fasten to the sides of the case, at top and bottom, with decorative brass stove bolts.

The thicknesses of the parts are listed as *nominally* ¾ inch, because I like the sidewalls and the unsupported shelves to be a bit thicker. The other parts can be a little thinner, if that's what it takes to get the best use out of the stock. The parts account for 3,508 square inches of material, which, allowing for normal waste, works up to just under 30 board feet. At current cherry prices, the project uses about $90 in wood. (Oak, ash, and maple will cost somewhat less, walnut about the same,

and mahogany slightly more, but there are sure to be some less expensive options!) This bookcase costs far less than all but the most generic particleboard-and-plastic imitations.

Construction Procedures

Cut, joint, and plane all pieces so they are slightly longer, wider, and thicker than indicated in the cutting list, checking their fits as you proceed. Then cut the slots for the biscuits and glue the biscuits into the individual pieces. My 10-inch-wide-panels all contain at *least* two biscuits, no single piece being over about 6 inches wide. I use many biscuits in a project like this, not so much for

Illus. 11-18.   This cherry bookcase can be quickly built and is collapsible for easy shipping.

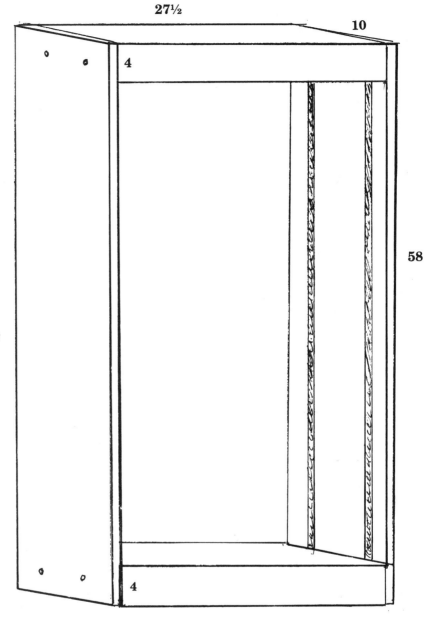

27½

10

4

58

4

4

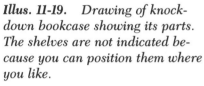

Illus. 11-19. *Drawing of knockdown bookcase showing its parts. The shelves are not indicated because you can position them where you like.*

Parts List for Knockdown Bookcase

Part	Length	Width	Thickness	Quantity
Shelves	27½″	10″	¾″	6
Sides of Main Assembly	58″	10″	¾″	2
Fronts and Backs of Sub-assembly	27½″	4″	¾″	4
Sides of Assembly	8½″	4″	¾″	4

Tools and Materials for Knockdown Bookcase
Biscuit joiner and biscuits
Table saw
Router
Layout tools
Clamps
Glue
Finishing products
4 pieces of 51-inch-long shelf standard
16 clips to match the standards
Eight ¼-inch × #20, 1½-inch-long brass roundhead stove bolts
Eight ¼-inch × #20 Tee-nuts, to mount on the insides

strength as for alignment. The biscuits for all these pieces were placed 3 inches from the ends and roughly 8 inches apart (measured by eye rather than with a ruler). Starting with rough stock, I glued up all panels in under three hours.

Remove glue meticulously. It is easier to do this while the glue is the consistency of cottage cheese than it is to do it after the glue has set!

Next, joint and plane the pieces to their final sizes. This will take less than an hour. Then make two boxes from the 4-inch-wide pieces, biscuiting their ends as shown in Illus. 11-20 and 11-21. Assemble these boxes on a very flat surface (like the top of your table saw, but put a sheet of wax paper over the table saw to protect the saw from glue squeeze-out). If you biscuit these boxes to-gether (Illus. 11-22), glue only in the biscuit slots. Tight biscuits may have to be tapped into the slot with a mallet.

Attach the top and bottom shelves to these boxes. With one edge biscuited flush, plane the other edge flush, and then apply the biscuits there (Illus. 11-23–11-25). I glued only one row of biscuits, wanting to leave some space for expansion and contraction.

Quarter-round the fronts and backs of both boxes (Illus. 11-26), the inside of the top box all the way around, and the outside of the top box at the front and back (Illus. 11-27).

Mark the insides for installing shelf standards. Use a router to cut a ⅝-inch-wide × ³⁄₁₆-inch-deep slot for the standards. I like the standards because

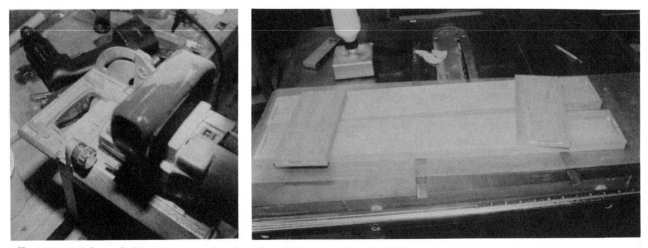

Illus. 11-20 (above left). Cutting the slots for the biscuits that hold the top and bottom boxes together. *Illus. 11-21 (above right).* The top and bottom boxes and side pieces ready to be glued and assembled.

Illus. 11-22. *The top and bottom boxes clamped to the sides.*

Illus. 11-23. *The framework biscuited to accept the top and bottom shelves.*

Illus. 11-24. *Glue the shelves to the framework.*

Illus. 11-25 (above left).   Put the biscuits in place on one side without gluing, set the shelf on the framework, and then plane it flush before cutting the slots for the biscuits on the other side of the shelf. Illus. 11-26 (above right). Quarter-round the fronts and backs of the boxes.

Illus. 11-27.   Quarter-round all around the inside of the top box as well as the front and back of the outside.

they are quick and neat to install. You can save some money by not using the shelf standards but instead drilling ¼-inch holes one inch apart in the same places that the four slots are routed, but the drilling will take an hour to do on a drill press.

After the slots have been routed, nailing the standards in place would seem the logical thing to do. Don't do it yet. Instead, do all your sanding and finishing, so that the area behind the shelf standards gets some finish.

I finished with Danish oil, of which Watco happens to be the brand I had available from a previous project (Illus. 11-28). There are many good brands of Danish oil available. My first coat of Danish oil goes on very wet, and I leave it there overnight. The next morning, there is a tacky

mess of undissolved oil on the surface. I reapply Danish oil to dissolve all that's drying on the surface, and wipe each piece very dry. By the next day, the wood will be ready to wax. I believe that one should follow a Danish oil treatment with the old cabinetmaker's formula for waxing: once a day for a week, once a week for a month, once a month for a year, and then, finally, once a year for all eternity. This has certainly left a very repairable finish on the furniture in my home.

Because sanding and finishing have removed all layout lines, assemble the top and bottom boxes to the sides before nailing the shelf standards in place. I made a jig for uniform drilling of the holes that mount the top and bottom (Illus. 11-29–11-31). I have drilled holes 2⅛ and 7⅞

Illus. 11-28.   Two of the shelves with Watco oil applied.

inches from the rear and 3 inches from the top or bottom. A ¾-inch spacer will be used on the top box to ensure that there is some space about the top. The jig is made from scrap plywood which has been glued and tacked together.

After the main carcass is assembled, install the standards. With hardwood, it is better to nail than to staple. At most hardware stores, you have to ask for the nails that come with the shelf standards. (Since the standards are bought in bulk, the nails are often not included.) Be sure you have more than ⅜ inch behind the standard to nail into or you'll have nails extending through the good side of the project.

As soon as the standards are in place, mount your shelves and give the bookcase its first coat of wax (Illus. 11-32 and 11-33). It won't be too long before you decide to make another.

Illus. 11-29.   The jig used to drill the assembly holes.

Illus. 11-30.   The jig in place for drilling the assembly holes.

Illus. 11-31.   Drilling the assembly holes.

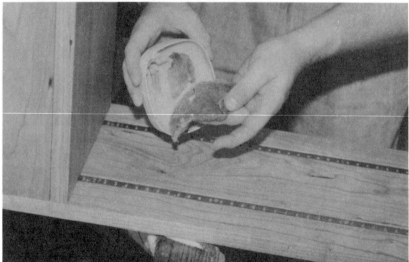

Illus. 11-32 and 11-33.   Applying the wax with a piece of Scotch-Brite pad.

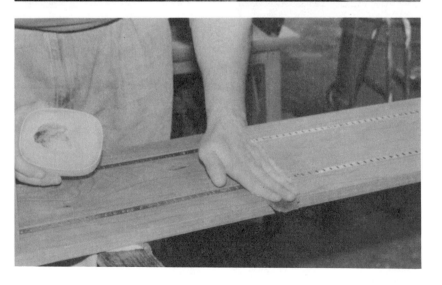

Illus. 11-33.

Illus. 11-34.   *The finished bookcase put to good use.*

Illus. 11-35.   *This stool can be quickly built and will prove to be useful around the house.*

A Handy Stool

This stool (Illus. 11-35–11-37) is another project that can be quickly built. It is sure to please people who reach to high places regularly. Building it is very easy. First, collect the wood you will use. Remember, all the pieces in the cutting list are nominally ¾ inch thick.

Next, cut the two 10-inches-wide × 9½-inches-long end pieces so that they are parallel to each other at 10 degrees off-square. Mark a 6-inch-wide × 5-inch-long rectangle, centering it at the bottom of each end. Then draw in the curve with an architect's curve (Illus. 11-38 and 11-39). Cut out these curves in one continuous single pass on the band saw. After you have cut both pieces, clamp them together and sand out the curves. Round over the edges of both the inside and the outside of the curves with your router and a ¼- or ⅜-inch roundover bit.

Illus. 11-36.   *Back view of the stool.*

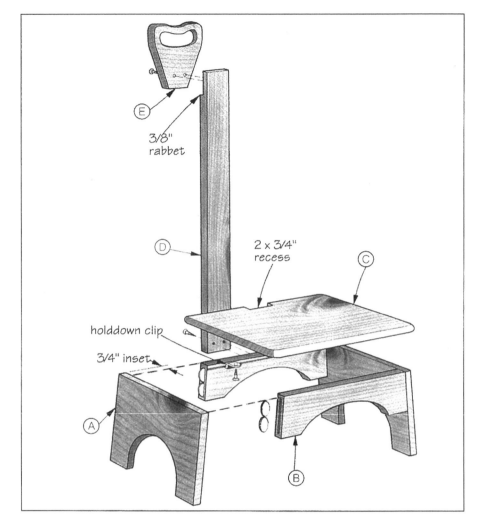

Illus. 11-37.   Drawing of stool showing its parts.

3/8"
rabbet

2 x 3/4"
recess

holddown clip

3/4" inset

Parts List for Stool

Label	Part	Length	Width	Thickness	Quantity
A	End	9½"	10"	¾"	2
B	Side	12½"	4¼"	¾"	2
C	Top	12½"	10"	¾"	1
D	Stretcher	26"	2"	¾"	1
E	Handle	6"	4"	¾"	1

Tools and Materials for Stool
Biscuit joiner and biscuits
Band saw
Router and ¼- or ⅜-inch roundover bit
Architect's curve
Screws and plugs
Table saw or router table
Layout tools
Clamps and glue

Illus. 11-38 and 11-39.   *Laying out the curves on the end pieces with an architect's curve.*

Illus. 11-39.

Next, cut the two side pieces. If you cut each end 10 degrees off-square, the side piece will be 12½ inches long at the bottom and 11 inches long at the top. Cut a ⅜-inch-deep kerf for the tabletop fasteners ½ inch from the top of the side piece. You will use the kerf to apply the top. Measure 2-inch-wide × 8½-inch-long rectangles in the middle of the bottom half of these side pieces. With the architect's curve, add a curve. Cut out the curve, sand the two pieces together, and round over the edges with the same router bit you used on the ends.

Next, with a random orbit sander (or another efficient sanding method available to you) sand all four pieces clean using sandpaper through 120 or 150 grit. Now, biscuit-join these four pieces to-gether (Illus. 11-40–11-42). One side should be joined ¾ inch from the edge of its end, to make room for the handle. Then use screws and plugs to reinforce these biscuit joints, just in case a user of the stool is very heavy.

On one face of your 10-inch-wide × 12½-inch-long top, cut a 2-inch-wide × ¾-inch-deep recess. This cut may be made on a table saw and then sanded, but you'll get much neater work if you cut the recess on a router table. Use a router bit to round all the faces of the top, except the ¾ inch at either end that contacts the base of the stool. Fasten the top of the base with fasteners like those available from the Woodworker's Store.

For the stretcher, cut a 2-inch-wide × 26-inch-long piece. Half-round all but the inside bottom

Illus. 11-40. *The pieces ready for assembly. I used 1½ biscuits to fill the joint.*

Illus. 11-41. *The glued-up assembly in the clamps. Note the protection offered by the blocks.*

Illus. 11-42. *A close-up of the glued assembly in the clamps shows the slot for the top-mounting hardware.*

2¾ inches of it. Using your table saw or router table, cut away half the thickness of the first 1 inch of the top, so that it can be attached to the handle. The space that is cleared here will be used to mount the handle. Then drill into the bottom two inches of this stretcher for a pair of screws which will attach this handle to the stool itself. Glue and screw the piece in place, and then cap or plug the screws.

Next, shape the handle to be as decorative as you want. I strongly recommend that the inside of the handle be the shape and size as indicated in the cutting list and shown in Illus. 11-43, and that you round it over on both sides before fastening it to the stretcher.

You'll find that several of these stools can be built pretty quickly (Illus. 11-44). That is a good thing, too, because when I gave this one to my mother, I was called by at least half a dozen of her friends who each wanted one.

Illus. 11-44.   *The stool against a background of fern.*

Desk Organizer

This desk organizer (Illus. 11-45 and 11-46) may just be what you need to get the clutter off your desk. That, at least, was my rationale for building the project. The best material for the organizer is the material that best matches the furnishings of the room it will be in. The desk organizer in Illus. 11-45 is built of cherry, but you could do as well with less expensive materials. If you are more concerned with how the desk organizer functions than how it looks, you could even use plywood such as Apple Ply or Baltic birch without having to tape the edges. If you're beginning with rough

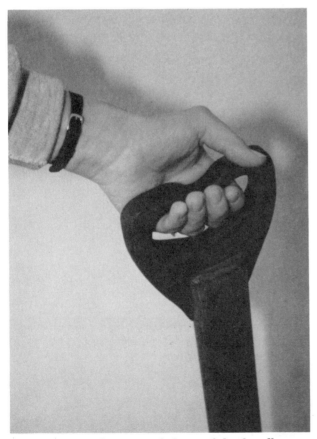

Illus. 11-43.   *The size and shape of this handle provide a comfortable hand grip.*

stock, joint and plane about 17 or 18 board feet. You may have a bit left over when the project is finished, but you'll definitely use this leftover material on future projects. If you're shopping for fresh stock, buy about 20 board feet and a small panel for the back.

This desk organizer did not take long to make. I spent part of one afternoon preparing stock and gluing it to width, part of another afternoon cut-ting the pieces to exact size, and a third afternoon assembling the unit, sanding it completely, and applying a coat of Danish oil.

It would be quite possible to add almost any number of shelves by altering my plan slightly. Whether you decide to use my plan completely or modify it, I'm sure you'll agree that this kind of system is better-looking than the plastic stuff that's so readily found in office-supply stores.

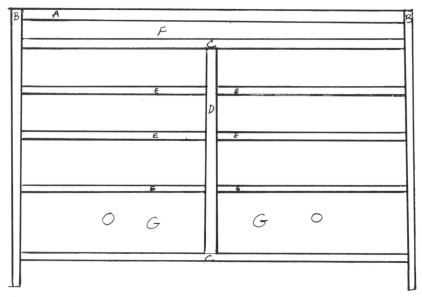

Illus. 11-45.   This desk organizer is built of cherry wood, but you can use less expensive materials. It will help you to better organize the papers in your office.

Illus. 11-46.   Drawing of desk organizer showing its parts. Parts H and I are not shown in the drawing, and F does not extend across the bottom of the desk organizer.

Parts List for Desk Organizer

Label	Part	Length	Width	Thickness	Quantity
A	Top Rail	30½"	1"	¾"	1
B	Side	23"	10"	¾"	2
C	Top and Bottom Shelves	30½"	10"	¾"	2
D	Center Upright	16"	9¾"	¾"	1
E	Shelf	14⅞"	9¾"	½"	6
F	Panel	31¼"	16¾"	¼"	1
G	Drawer Front and Back (Each Drawer)	14¾"	3⁷⁄₁₆"	½"	2
H	Drawer Sides (Each Drawer)	9¾"	3⁷⁄₁₆"	½"	2
I	Drawer Bottom (Each Drawer)	14"	9"	⅛"	1

Tools and Materials for Desk Organizer

Joiner/planer
Table saw or other power saw
Biscuit joiner with biscuits
Layout tools (rule, square, pencil)
Chisels
Dovetail saw
Clamps
Sander (preferably belt, random orbit, or finishing sander)
Router with ⅜-inch rabbet bit
Carpenter's glue

Construction Procedures

Start by preparing stock. After jointing and planing the pieces, cut them to length and measure them for final width. After you're sure the stock is squarely planed, glue the pieces together to get the desired 10-inch widths. I use three or four biscuits per glue-up.

Illus. 11-47–11-50 show stock preparation and gluing. Note that I used a very light film of glue on each mating surface. The goal is to get some squeeze-out when the assembly is clamped even with light clamping pressure, but not so much

Illus. 11-47. Using the joiner to ensure alignment when gluing up stock for the various panels in the project.

Illus. 11-48. Note the glue on the mating surfaces and in the biscuit slots.

Illus. 11-50. This small stack of panels is the product of the gluing operation.

Illus. 11-49. Use plenty of clamps when gluing up the panels.

squeeze-out that there is a mess. I used a total of 24 biscuits to glue the pieces to the width needed. If you don't have a dozen or more clamps, your project may go more slowly than it did in my shop.

After the stock has been cut to size, lay out the biscuit joints (Illus. 11-51 and 11-52). Measure down 2½ inches from the tops of the sides and scribe a line. (It is recommended that woodworkers scribe lines with a knife or similar tool,

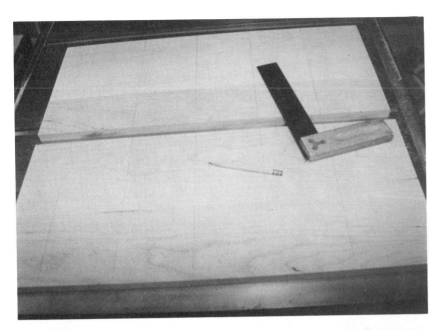

Illus. 11-51 and 11-52.
The layout for the T-joints.

Illus. 11-52.

but when biscuit-joining use a *soft* pencil. The marks should be dark enough to be clearly visible, but they should be easy to remove.) Do this again 6½, 10½, 14½, and 18½ inches from the top.

Next, starting at the bottom of the assembly, clamp the crosspiece to the side ends, and then scribe marks for the joiner 2½ inches from either end and in the middle of the crosspiece (Illus. 11-53). With the flap face removed from the joiner, cut first three horizontal slots, and then three vertical slots (Illus. 11-54–11-57). Do this to the

other end of the assembly. Repeat the joint with the other 30½-inch-long piece, the top rail.

The flip-flop T-joint method is the preferred fastening method for each of the joints in this project. I measured T-joints across the board at 2½, 5, and 7½ inches.

Use a piece of like-thickness stock when cutting at the short end of a board. Cut the slots in both ends of the full-width top and bottom shelves. Then insert two dry biscuits in each joint and test the assembly. While the assembly is together like

Illus. 11-53.   Clamp the boards so that the "shelves" meet the lines drawn on the sidewalls.

Illus. 11-54 and 11-55.   Two views showing how the material should be clamped for the horizontal and vertical cuts.

Illus. 11-55.

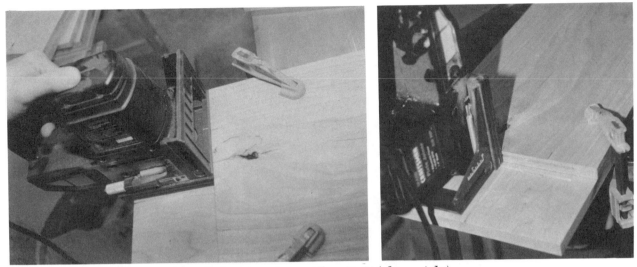

Illus. 11-56 (above left).   *Making the horizontal cuts. Illus. 11-57 (above right).*
Making the vertical cuts.

this, check the exact length for the center-divider piece (D in Illus. 11-46). Crosscut it to length with your table saw, and then repeat the biscuit joints as above. Make another dry assembly, now with this center piece in place. Measure the centerlines so they correspond to the middle three lines on the outer walls of the piece.

Cut the six center shelves so they are the exact length to fit between the outer and middle walls. Then apply the biscuits to these slots using exactly the same techniques described above, that is,

applying biscuits at either side of each of these six pieces.

If the pieces fit precisely when you dry-fit them, sand them as completely as you feel is needed. I sanded each piece with a random orbit sander using sandpaper up through 120 grit, applied glue to the biscuit slots only, and reassembled the project (Illus. 11-58 and 11-59). Be sure to align the front edges when assembling the pieces, so that the middle pieces and the top shelf are inset by ¼ inch. I used a router with a ⅜-inch

Illus. 11-58 and 11-59 (following page).   *Clamp the glued and biscuited project together. Note that clamps are used vertically and horizontally.*

Illus. 11-59.

Illus. 11-60.   Squaring the routed back-panel rabbet with a chisel.

rabbet bit to make most of the channel in the back and sides. One could certainly cut the rabbet in the bottom shelf before applying it, and that would make cutting the rabbet in the sidewalls much easier. After routing the channel, square off the channels with a chisel (Illus. 11-60). This makes it easier to cut a piece of plywood to fit.

I added a piece of ¾- × 1-inch trim across the top back. All that really holds this piece in place is a snug fit and a few drops of judiciously placed glue.

Next, I built a pair of drawers from ½-inch-thick material. The dimensions for the drawers in the cutting list are for drawers that have been hand-dovetailed together. If you are going to biscuit-join the drawers, make the side pieces 1 inch shorter. Biscuit-joined drawers will be a bit quicker to make and perhaps equally strong, but

they may not be quite as attractive (Illus. 11-61 and 11-62). The slots are routed in the drawer sides for the bottoms. These slots could be cut on the table saw, but the slots on the front and back pieces shouldn't be cut all the way to the edges of the material. I routed these slots ¼ inch deep by just over ⅛ inch wide, and used ⅛-inch-thick plywood for the bottoms. The desk organizer shown in the illustrations has ⅛-inch-thick cherry plywood bottoms, but the project would work just fine with ⅛-inch-thick pressed board (sometimes sold generically as Masonite).

After you have completed the assembly of both the main body of the project and the drawers (Illus. 11-63) and let the glue dry, chip away any glue bubbles and complete the sanding process. While a pad finishing sander might be desirable for the outside and top edges and for the fronts of the shelves, the insides of the shelves can be sanded just fine by hand. I seldom sand a project past 150-to-180-grit sandpaper, for my experience is that a surface sanded with 220-grit sandpaper is too smooth for the Danish oil finish I prefer to dry satisfactorily.

After a couple of coats of Danish oil and some wax, the office organizer is ready to be put to work. It is not advisable to apply a finish like Danish oil to the inside of the drawers, for it will leave the drawers smelling permanently of it.

Illus. 11-63.   A single drawer in place.

Illus. 11-61 and 11-62.   Two views of the biscuit joint that holds the drawer together.

As soon as you're certain that your finish has dried, the desk organizer is ready to take to your office. This is a project that will remain useful for quite a long time to come.

Car-Top Carrier

A friend of mine asked me to help him build a "casket" to carry his skis in (Illus. 11-64 and 11-65). We made a quick analysis of what was needed, and my friend bought a sheet and a half of very inexpensive ½-inch-thick plywood with which to build the carrier. This plywood wasn't very flat at all, and it took judicious use of biscuit joinery to bring the parts of the carrier square.

Construction Procedures

Following are the techniques we used to make the car-top carrier:

First, we cut the parts out with a table saw. We used the table saw to rip the plywood to 23⅞ inches wide, because there is no way to get two 24-inch-wide pieces out of a 48-inch sheet. At what became the front end of the top and bottom pieces, we cut a 45-degree edge mitre so that when the sides with 45-degree frame mitres were

Illus. 11-62.

added, the opening would present a flat plane to the door we would add. Cutting the 45-degree frame mitres on the wide pieces was easy work with a sliding compound mitre saw, although this operation could be readily done with a 45-degree setting on a table saw's mitre gauge or by carefully laying out and cutting the mitre with a handsaw.

We placed the four large pieces together and laid out the biscuit joints. We made the first layout lines 2½ inches from each end, and about a hand's-width apart in between (Illus. 11-66). The unit is held together with corner-butt joints that are close together and with glue. Illus. 11-67 shows how close the corner butt-joint interval is.

Cutting the vertical slots was pretty easy (Illus. 11-68 and 11-69) because I had a joiner with a flap fence. It was simply a matter of setting the flap to 90 degrees and plunging the blade directly into

Illus. 11-64. *This car-top ski carrier was built with a sheet and a half of ½-inch-thick plywood.*

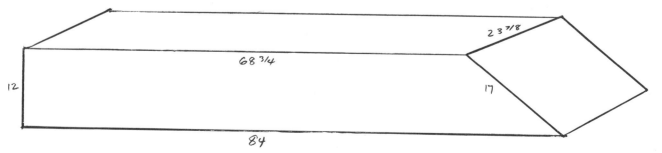

Illus. 11-65. *Drawing of car-top ski carrier.*

Parts List for Car-Top Carrier

Part or Material	Length	Width	Thickness	Quantity
Bottom (The 45-degree edge mitre is cut at what will be the "front" end.)	84"	23⅞"	½"	1
Top (The 45-degree edge mitre is cut at what will be the "front" end.)	68¾"	23⅞"	½"	1
Back Door (Cut it square.)	12"	23⅞"	½"	1
Front Door (Cut parallel 45-degree edge mitres at its top and bottom. Also, measure your assembled sides, top, and bottom before cutting to be sure their lengths are precisely what you want.)	17"	23⅞"	½"	1
Sides (The "front" end of each piece is cut with 45-degree frame mitres, so the front door will fit flush over the ends.)	84"	12"	½"	2
Hinges (Choose the type that you feel will work best for you.)				2 pairs
Hasps (padlock closures)				2

Tools and Materials for Car-Top Carrier
Biscuit joiner and approximately 40 biscuits
Table saw
Glue
Layout tools
Clamps

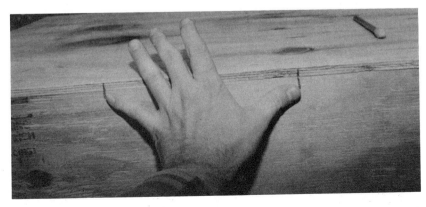

Illus. 11-66. Lay out the joints about a hand's-width apart.

Illus. 11-67.   The layout lines for the corner butt joints are quite close to one another.

Illus. 11-68.   The vertical cuts are being made by holding a corner of the joiner's flap face with the thumb of one hand, to ensure that it is squarely against the face of the work.

Illus. 11-69.   Make sure that the stabilizing hand is not in the vicinity of the cut.

the edge grain of the plywood. After these slots were all cut, we cut the matching slots on the horizontal pieces (Illus. 11-70 and 11-71). These pieces are sometimes more difficult to cut slots in squarely, but a bit of practice and patience will usually prevail. In many ways, cutting this joint would be easier with a nonflap joiner, because without the flap we'd be more likely to use the smaller sliding square on the standard joiner. Note that hearing protection should be worn and a dust-collection system used whenever using power tools.

After the slots have all been cut, test-fit the joints with biscuits before gluing, and then glue all the slots and edges to be joined. Apply the biscuits quickly and clamp the project. Since this project was going to be painted rather than stained or simply coated with clear finish, we just wiped the excess glue up with paper towels. After the unit had sat in clamps for 30 minutes, we took

Illus. 11-71.   A close-up of cutting the slots on the horizontal pieces.

the clamps off, cleaned up the edges a bit, and my friend took the project home. He put a screw that extended through the bottom of the casket to a pair of 2 × 4s that attached directly to the car-top carrier. He added two pairs of hinges that open from the top and hasps (padlock closures) to complete the unit. After a couple of coats of exterior paint, he had a means of transporting his skis to the slopes. I suspect his unit will hold quite literally dozens of skis—enough skis for far more people than his automobile will carry to the slopes.

Illus. 11-70.   Maintaining stability is even more challenging on the horizontal cut.

Chest with a "Carved" Shell

The inspiration for this project (Illus. 11-72 and 11-73) is a dark-stained antique piece I saw in a restaurant. The piece had a full-length back, and the front of the unit was simply nailed or screwed to it from behind. As handsome as this piece was, I felt that I could build a better, equally attractive one that the hobbyist woodworker would also like to build.

The original chest was made of ¾-inch-thick stock, which is standard thickness for dimension lumber, and was built with pine, so if your best source of material is dimension lumber from a nearby lumberyard or home center, refer to the cutting list for ¾-inch-thick stock on page 118. If you prefer to plane your own stock, you might as well use a finer hardwood and let the beauty of the material stand out rather than cover it up with a heavy stain job. If you're planing your own stock, you can build the project of mainly ½-inch-thick material (like the cherry-wood piece shown in Illus. 11-72) by using the cutting list on page 119. This is the plan I've followed, using ¾-inch stock only for the shell.

If you make the project from ½-inch-thick stock as I did, you'll use approximately 18 board feet, which includes a fairly generous allowance of just over 20 percent for waste. By multiplying the board footage by your per-board-foot cost, you'll know ahead of time what the project will cost. My cherry chest cost about $70, including knobs, abrasives, and finishing materials.

On the chest shown in Illus. 11-72, I have used Woodcraft Supply 1¼-inch Shaker-style cherry knobs. However, it would be perfectly acceptable to use other knobs or pulls that are available locally.

Construction Procedures

Because the pieces are relatively small, use a table saw to crosscut the rough lumber to form pieces that are somewhat longer than called for, for easier jointing and planing. After jointing one face and one edge, cut the pieces one jointer pass wider than their finished widths. By cutting before surfacing, you ensure that you're not wasting surfacing time.

One way of making the "carved" shell without actually carving it is to make a series of angled pieces, and to round each piece over with a router and a ⅜-inch router bit (Illus. 11-74). People who don't carve are sure to find this easier than actually carving the shell. Assembling the shell in this way (Illus. 11-75) also provides an opportunity to mix wood species. For example, bird's-eye maple and cherry look very good together, as do walnut and cherry. Cherry alone presents a myriad of possibilities, and my model shows many of them. Why would anyone want to stain a project that has this much natural beauty?

Illus. 11-72. The chest shown here was built of ½-inch-thick stock, and the shell of ¾-inch-thick stock. It is made of cherry.

A pencil line along the fence side of the table-saw blade greatly eases set-ups for cutting pieces like the angle pieces that will make up the shell (A in Illus. 11-73). I cut 18 angled pieces, quarter-rounded them on two edges, and then cut slots in them for #10 biscuits. It's wise—and safe—to clamp each piece as you do this. I did the routing freehand, resting the router on a block that's the same thickness as the pieces being routed. However, this is a job better suited for a router table and a couple of push sticks.

After the shell biscuits—and only the biscuits—have been glued, set a stack of wood on top of the shell to ensure that it stays flat while the glue sets (Illus. 11-76). Set a layer of wax paper between the saw table and this shell, and another layer between the work and the stack of wood.

Only after this shell has been made should you start making the chest's carcass. Cut the side vertical pieces 6 inches wide by 19¾ inches long. Set the two pieces down *inside side up* parallel to one another. Clamp their ends together to ensure an

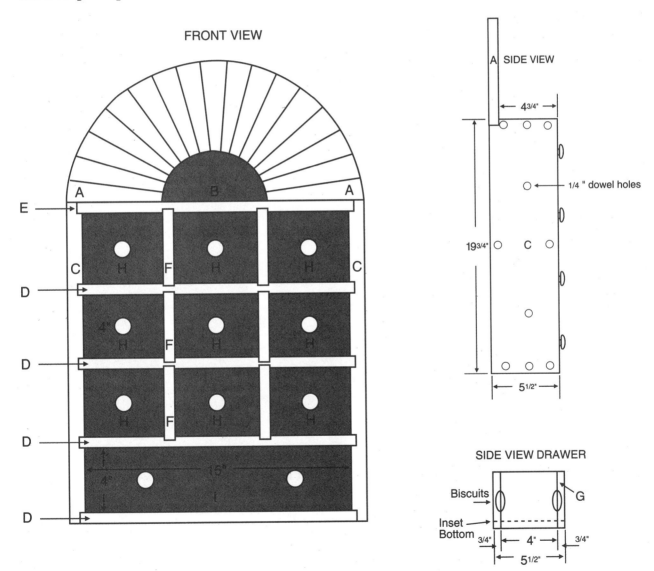

Illus. 11-73. Drawing of chest with "carved" shell.

Parts List for Chest with "Carved" Shell When Using ¾-Inch-Thick Stock

Parts List for Carcass

Label	Part	Length	Width	Thickness	Quantity
C	Side Vertical Piece	19¾"	6"	¾"	2
D	Horizontal Piece	15"	6"	¾"	4
E	Horizontal Piece for Top	15"	5¼"	¾"	1
A	Shell (You only need this piece if you're carving the shell from a single piece.)	15"	8¼"	¾"	1

Parts List for One Drawer (I in Illus. 11-73)

Part	Length	Width	Thickness	Quantity
Front and Back	13½"	4"	¾"	2
Side	4½"	4"	¾"	2
Plywood Bottom	12¾"	5¼"	⅛" or ¼"	1
Cherry Knob (commercially available)			⅞" or 1⅛"	2

Parts List for Nine Drawers Shown as H in Illus. 11-73. (Quantities Are for One Drawer.)

Part	Length	Width	Thickness	Quantity
Side	5"	4¼"	½"	2
Front and Back	4¼"	4¼"	½"	2
Plywood Bottom	5½"	4¾"	⅛" or ¼"	1
Cherry Knob (commerically available)			⅞" or 1⅛"	1

Parts List for Shell (A and B in Illus. 11-73)

Part	Length	Width	Thickness	Quantity
Half-round Piece for Center	4"	2"	¾"	1
Shell Piece (Each piece is tapered to ⅝ inch wide at one end for fan.)	7"	2⅝"	¾"	10

Parts List for Chest with "Carved" Shell
When Using ½-Inch-Thick Stock

Parts List for Carcass

Label	Part	Length	Width	Thickness	Quantity
C	Vertical Piece	19¾"	6"	½"	2
D	Horizontal Piece	15"	6"	½"	4
E	Horizontal piece for Top	15"	5¼"	½"	1
A and B	Shell (You need this piece only if you're carving the shell from a single piece.)	15"	8"	¾"	1
F	Vertical Dividers	4½"	6"	½"	6

Parts List for One Drawer (I in Illus. 11-73)

Part	Length	Width	Thickness	Quantity
Front and Back	14"	4¼"	½"	2
Side	5"	4¼"	½"	2
Plywood Bottom	13½"	5½"	⅛" or ¼"	1
Cherry Knob (commerically available)			⅞" or 1⅛"	2

Parts List for Nine Drawers Shown as H in Illus. 11-73
(Quantities Are for One Drawer.)

Part	Length	Width	Thickness	Quantity
Side	4"	4"	¾"	2
Front and Back	4½"	4"	¾"	2
Bottom (plywood)	5¼"	3¼"	⅛" or ¼"	1
Cherry Knob (commerically available)			⅞" or 1⅛"	1

Parts List for Shell (A & B in Illus. 11-73)

Part	Length	Width	Thickness	Quantity
Half-round Piece for Center	4"	2"	¾"	1
Shell Piece (Each piece tapered to ⅝ inch wide at one end for fan)	7"	2⅝"	¾"	10

Tools and Materials for Chest with "Carved" Shell
Biscuit joiner and biscuits
Table saw
Abrasives and finishing materials
Layout tools
Clamps
Router

Illus. 11-74 (left).   *Rounding over the curves on the shell pieces.*

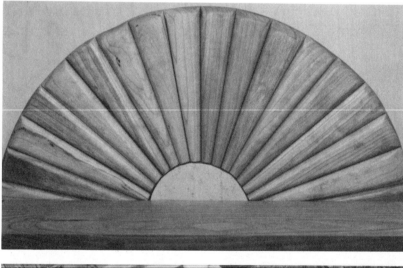

Illus. 11-75.   *A close-up of the assembled shell. Assembling the shell by cutting a series of angled pieces and rounding each piece over with a router allows you to combine different wood species to create a stunning effect.*

Illus. 11-76.   *Holding the completed shell in place.*

accurate layout. Lay out lines for rabbets half an inch from the top and bottom.

Next, measure 4⁵⁄₁₆ inches up the pieces and scribe a line. Then measure and scribe another line ½ inch above the first one (Illus. 11-77). Illus. 11-78 shows a line made with a rule and another line made by holding a piece of ½-inch-thick stock in place. I'll trust my rule, thanks!

Repeat the two steps in the above paragraph each twice. After you have done this, there should

be four areas, each 4⁵⁄₁₆ inches long, and rabbet or dado spots for five crosspieces.

Illus. 11-79. Setting the router bit's depth of cut for cutting dadoes in the drawer runners.

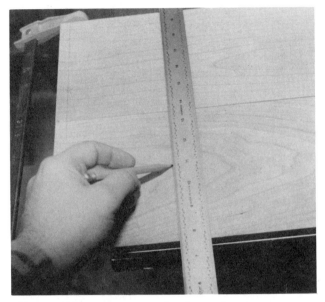

Illus. 11-77. Laying out the drawer's runners.

Illus. 11-78. The line on the inside was made with a ruler, and the other line was made with a piece of ½-inch-thick stock. The ruler seems to be more reliable.

Illus. 11-80. A wood guide is clamped precisely three inches from one of the marked or scribed lines.

Next, insert a ½-inch bit in your router and set the depth of cut for ³⁄₁₆ inch (Illus. 11-79). Clamp a guide precisely three inches from one of your marked lines (Illus. 11-80). Cut the rabbets and dadoes across these pieces which will form the vertical side pieces (Illus. 11-81).

Illus. 11-81.
Cutting the slots across the pieces that will form the side pieces.

You can proceed to cut the dadoes in the horizontal pieces with your router and its ½-inch bit, but it may be faster to cut them on a table saw with a dado set. After very carefully setting up the width and depth of cut, and making several test cuts, set the mitre gauge so that each piece to be dadoed could be done from the same setting. Cut one end, and then flip the piece to cut the other end.

Cut a total of 12 dadoes 4¹³⁄₁₆ inches from each end. Cut two on the underside of the top, four on each of the two middle shelves (two on the top and two on the bottom), and two on the upper side of the bottom interior piece.

After all these cuts have been made, dry-assemble the carcass and cut the six dividers to fit. If you're working accurately, these pieces should all be 4¹¹⁄₁₆ inches. Measure before you cut each piece, so you cut pieces you can actually use rather than pieces that conform to a plan. If your cutting is even just slightly off, you'll find yourself straying from the dimension of the pieces by ¹⁄₃₂ inch or so.

Fit these dividers into place and trim them to fit with a block plane. The unit is now ready for assembly (Illus. 11-82). At this time, do any and all power sanding you want done to the interior surfaces. After the unit has been assembled, even hand-sanding the interiors will be challenging. I assembled the carcass with glue and dowels. On the bottom interior divider, I used several wood screws in lieu of dowels.

After gluing and clamping the carcass, drill for ¼-inch dowels. I drilled three dowels at the top and bottom, two at the center shelf, and one on each of the other two shelves. Single dowels were centered. When two were used, one was placed one inch from either side of the board. When three were used, one was centered and the other two were placed one inch from the side of the

Illus. 11-82.   *Clamping the carcass helps to ensure that it stays perfectly square while the glue sets.*

board. Using 20 pieces of 1¼-inch-long dowels means that the entire project can be completed with a single 36-inch-long dowel. I cut the dowel into several pieces, inserted the dowel pieces, and then cut it flush with a Japanese saw, which is the ideal tool for the job.

Sand the sides and top of the carcass. Cut the back ¾ inch off the top, so you can fasten the shell to the top. Lay the shell in place, drill some pilot holes, and screw the shell and its slightly off-center center to the top shelf.

If the unit is to be wall-hung, this is as good a time as any to mount your hanging hardware. I mounted a pair of wire end hangers to the back of the unit at the height of the second shelf (Illus. 11-83). To keep the hanging unit parallel to the wall, I added a pair of rubber bumpers to the bottom back corners (Illus. 11-84). These are common hardware items that I buy in my local hardware store.

Illus. 11-83.   I mounted wire end hangers to the back of the chest at the height of the second shelf.

Illus. 11-84.   A pair of rubber bumpers were added to the bottom back corners of the chest. These bumpers helped keep the hanging unit parallel to the wall.

Now, it's time to make the drawers. In this project, the drawers are biscuit-joined together. Start by cutting 20 pieces that are 4¼ inches wide × 5 inches long to use as drawer sides. Then cut 18 pieces the same width × 4½ inches long and two pieces the same width × 14½ inches long for use as fronts and backs for the drawers.

Plan your cutting carefully so that you can continue the pattern of a board across the series of three drawers. Note that the top and bottom rows of drawers in the chest illustrated do this—and both look better than the middle row, where the continuing piece got lost somehow. Use your biscuit joiner to form simple butt joints.

Test-fit the drawers together. If any sanding is needed on the inside sides of these drawers, now is the time (Illus. 11-85). After the drawers have been assembled, it will be too late!

Illus. 11-85.   Sanding a drawer.

Cut the drawer bottoms. You'll need nine pieces 3⅞ inches wide × 5½ inches long and one piece 5½ inches wide × 13⅞ inches long. I made mine from some ⅛-inch-thick lauan mahogany plywood that I rescued from a shipping crate, but ⅛-inch-thick Masonite would work as well.

Cut the slots for the drawer bottoms with a table saw or with a router and a ⅛-inch router bit. Use the router bit if you object to the small visible kerf shown in Illus. 11-86. I've made the sample this way in an attempt to keep the project as simple as possible.

Since you've dry-fitted all the drawers with biscuits in place, you'll have to remove them for cutting the slots for the bottoms. A ⅛-inch chisel can ease out these biscuits quite effectively. I laid each drawer out with its bottom inside facing up and towards the center. This way, I was reminded of the proper sequence for picking up the pieces for slotting (Illus. 11-86).

Illus. 11-86.   This glimpse of the bottom of a drawer shows how it would look if you were to cut slots the full length of the drawer's bottom.

Assemble the drawers (Illus. 11-87). Be sure you have 40 #10 biscuits ready for use. Glue the drawers together only in the biscuit slots. That really helps to keep the project neat. Be sure to clamp each glued drawer.

After the glue has set, sand each drawer and mark them for the knobs. Drill a hole 2¼ inches from the bottom of the exact middle of each drawer. I did this in a drill press, although these holes could probably have been drilled by hand just as well. After setting a drop of glue on the post of the knobs, drive them home. If you want the insides of the drawers to look as good as possible, cut off approximately ³⁄₁₆ inch of the posts. It might be wise to check the size of your knobs' posts with a dowel sizer. As I forced home a knob with an oversized post, I cracked the drawer, and then broke the knob as I attempted to extract it.

As soon as the pulls are on the drawers, they and the carcass are ready for final hand-sanding. Sand the parts completely and do whatever adjusting is necessary to make the project as perfect as possible. Then apply your finish. I've used only half a dozen coats of clear water-based polyurethane varnish because I wanted to give the project a natural look as much as I wanted to protect the project. It seems to me that Danish oil should not be used because it is likely to turn rancid and emit an odor in these enclosed drawers.

Illus. 11-87.   Put glue only in the biscuit slots while assembling the drawers.

Illus. 11-88.   The completed project.

GLOSSARY

Apron   A downward extension on a piece of furniture that connects the legs.

Base   The underside of the machine. Good-quality bases have layout lines which help to position the cuts.

Bevel   An inclined, angled, or slanted edge.

Biscuit Joiner (also referred to as a plate joiner)   A grinder-like device with a spring-loaded faceplate that sets for plunge-cutting slots. Biscuits are then used to join the slots cut by the joiner.

Biscuits (also referred to as splines or plates).   Thin, elliptical wooden wafers that are used to join the slots or grooves cut by the joiner. Biscuits commonly come in sizes #0, #10, and #20, with the #20 biscuits arguably the most commonly used. Lamello has introduced three new sizes of biscuits in recent years: #4, #6, and #H9. There are also accessory biscuits available used for specialized jobs such as for knock-down furniture.

Blind Joint   A joint cut only partially through the board so that the end grain is hidden.

Butt Joint   A joint in which the edge or end of one board is butted against a face of another board.

Carcass   The basic frame of a cabinet.

Chipboard   A paperboard usually made entirely from wastepaper.

Corian   Man-made stone sold as (very expensive) sheet stock. Other brands of similar products include Avonite and Fountainhead.

Crosscut   A cutting across or against the grain of wood.

Dado Blade   The blade used on a table saw to cut dado joints.

Dado Joint   A T-shaped joint used to make boxes, cabinets, and shelves, where the perpendicular piece rides in a groove (dado) cut into the other piece with a saw, router, or by hand with a saw and a chisel.

D-Handle   A handle found on the front of virtually all joiners which is basically shaped like the letter D. Recently, Lamello has made standard a "universal handle," which is much more comfortable to use.

Depth of Cut   The amount of stock the biscuit-joiner blade cuts when controlled by the depth-of-cut adjustment.

Dovetail Joint   A joint in which tapered pins fit into sockets between flared tails.

Dowel   A butt joint is reinforced with wooden pegs called dowels. A dowel is used in cabinets and bookcases and to join the parts of a chair or table legs to a rail. These joints are largely rendered obsolete by biscuit joinery.

Edge Grain   The fibre orientation of the board edge.

Edge Joint   A joint used to join the edge of one board to the face of another. Edge joints are often used when applying trim or face frames to a cabinet.

Edge of Stock   The narrower surface of a board which runs parallel with the grain on the face of the board.

End Grain   The porous ends of wood fibre.

Face of Stock   The wider surface of a board, on which more grain is visible.

Face Frame   The face structure in a piece of furniture that is composed of horizontal and vertical pieces that form the openings for drawers and doors.

Faceplate   The plate on the front of the joiner. The blade plunges through the faceplate to make the cut for the slot.

Fence   The square or angled (usually at 45 degrees)

attachment to the joiner's faceplate which helps determine the position of the joiner's slotting cuts.

Gauge Blocks   Shop-made accessories that help to set up the biscuit joiner for squarely positioned cuts.

Glue Bottle   A bottle made for gluing biscuit joints. It has a nozzle that spreads the glue on the sides of the slots rather than in the bottoms.

Grain Direction   The orientation of the fibres in the wood.

Hardboard   A sheet material made by compressing wood fibres.

Jointer   A tool used to surface or level rough lumber.

Knockdown Furniture   Furniture that can be easily assembled or taken apart. Biscuit joints are used frequently in knockdown furniture.

Layout (also sometimes referred to as marking out).   The act of making the pencil marks which indicate where the biscuits will be placed. This may be quickly or carefully done, but if it isn't done the pieces aren't likely to be properly aligned at assembly. Accurate setup is the key to accurate joining.

Marking Gauge   A tool used to lay out lines parallel to the edges of a board.

Mitre Gauge   The part of a table saw that slides into the mitre slot, which is cut into the table and runs parallel to the saw blade. The mitre gauge is used to control stock when it is being cut.

Mitre Joint   A joint made by fastening together usually perpendicular pieces with ends cut at an angle.

Mortise-and-Tenon Joint   A joint in which a projection on one board called a tongue fits into a groove on another board.

Moulding   A wood-surface shape or a narrow strip that is used primarily for decoration.

Offset Joints   Joints that are cut with a shim between the fence of the biscuit joiner and the face of one of the pieces of material being cut. A prime example of an offset joint is the joint where the table legs meet the apron.

Particleboard   A sheet material made from pressed wood chips or wood particles.

Plywood   A sheet material made by gluing together thin layers of wood.

PVA (Polyvinyl Acetate) Glue   Sometimes called white glue, this is the most common variety of woodworking glue. It is commonly used to glue biscuits. Its moisture causes biscuits to swell, which makes for a stronger joint.

Rabbet Joint   An L-shaped joint that goes along the edge of a piece of stock. The perpendicular piece of the joint is mounted in a rabbet on the other piece. This rabbet is a dado that is open on one side.

Rip Fence   An accessory on the table saw that is used to control stock when you are ripping, that is, cutting with the grain.

Sandpaper   A coated abrasive with a paper backing.

Sheet Stock   Any wood material sold in sheets 4 feet wide and 8 to 12 feet long. Common types of sheet stock include particleboard, plywood, panelling, and hardboard.

Spline   A thin piece of wood that fits into a groove that is cut into both mating surfaces of a joint.

Square   To ensure that the parts are at perfect right (90-degree) angles to each other.

T-Joints   Butt joints used on internal pieces as support members to strengthen a frame. They are ideal to use on fixed-position shelves and dividers.

Tongue-and-Groove Joint   A joint in which a projection on one board called a tongue fits into a groove on the next board.

Workpiece   The piece of wood that is being cut or worked.

METRIC CHART

mm—millimetres   **cm—centimetres**

INCHES TO MILLIMETRES AND CENTIMETRES

inches	mm	cm	inches	cm	inches	cm
⅛	3	0.3	9	22.9	30	76.2
¼	6	0.6	10	25.4	31	78.7
⅜	10	1.0	11	27.9	32	81.3
½	13	1.3	12	30.5	33	83.8
⅝	16	1.6	13	33.0	34	86.4
¾	19	1.9	14	35.6	35	88.9
⅞	22	2.2	15	38.1	36	91.4
1	25	2.5	16	40.6	37	94.0
1¼	32	3.2	17	43.2	38	96.5
1½	38	3.8	18	45.7	39	99.1
1¾	44	4.4	19	48.3	40	101.6
2	51	5.1	20	50.8	41	104.1
2½	64	6.4	21	53.3	42	106.7
3	76	7.6	22	55.9	43	109.2
3½	89	8.9	23	58.4	44	111.8
4	102	10.2	24	61.0	45	114.3
4½	114	11.4	25	63.5	46	116.8
5	127	12.7	26	66.0	47	119.4
6	152	15.2	27	68.6	48	121.9
7	178	17.8	28	71.1	49	124.5
8	203	20.3	29	73.7	50	127.0

Index